MAYER ON THE

Mayer on the Media

Issues and Arguments

Henry Mayer
Edited by Rodney Tiffen

AFTRS

ALLEN & UNWIN

First published in 1994 by
Allen & Unwin Pty Ltd
9 Atchison Street, St Leonards, NSW 2065 Australia
in conjunction with the Australian Film Television & Radio School
North Ryde, NSW 2113 Australia

National Library of Australia
Cataloguing-in-Publication entry:

Mayer, Henry, 1919– .
Mayer on the media.

Bibliography.
Includes index.
ISBN 1 86373 625 5 (Allen & Unwin).

1. Mass media. 2. Mass media — Australia. I. Tiffen, Rodney.
II. Australian Film, Television and Radio School. III. Title.

302.23

Set in 11/12 pt Garamond by DOCUPRO, Sydney
Printed and bound in Australia by McPherson's Printing Pty Ltd

10 9 8 7 6 5 4 3 2 1

Contents

Acknowledgments

The primary purpose of this volume is to make some seminal writings of Henry Mayer easily available to all those interested in Australian media issues in the 1990s. For both those who knew Henry and his work, and to a new generation, these contributions will be fresh and pertinent to contemporary issues and debates.

Secondarily, I hope that many of those who were colleagues and friends of Henry, and also of mine, will like the collection. I think of members of the Department of Government at the University of Sydney, particularly Ross Curnow, Helen Nelson, Michael Leigh, Trevor Matthews, Michael Hogan, Ken Turner, Ian Grosart and Terry Irving; of those who had the mixed blessing of working for Henry, especially Sue Irving, Betty Johnson and Liz Kirby; of those who did post-graduate work with Henry, including Elaine Thompson, Sue Wills, Neville Petersen and especially Kate Harrison; of those who have combined an intellectual engagement with media issues with personal policy involvements, particularly Peter Westerway, Mark Armstrong and Julie James Bailey; of the countless media scholars throughout Australia who have had fruitful relationships with Henry, but particularly my colleagues who continue his work on *Media Information Australia*: Meredith Quinn, Stuart Cunningham, Liz Jacka, John Sinclair, Peter White, Richard Harris and especially Murray Goot, who compiled the invaluable, annotated bibliography of Henry's writings up to 1985; of Henry's early colleagues in building the study of Australian politics, especially Joan Rydon who, with Murray, edited the special issue of *Politics* when Henry retired. Most particularly I think of Elaine and Vicky Mayer.

The original sources of the chapters in this book are listed in the bibliography at its end. I wish to acknowledge all those who kindly gave their permission to reproduce them here.

The editing has sought to retain the viewpoints and flavour of the original articles. The main editing has been to delete references to what were then recent developments and current scholarly writings, but which no longer hold strong contemporary interest.

The royalties from this book will go to the Henry Mayer Trust, a group whose purpose is to support those scholarly activities on Australian media to which Henry devoted so much of his life.

Introduction

Rodney Tiffen

Henry Mayer was unlike any other media scholar. Everything about him was arresting—his imposing presence, his passionate scepticism, his iconoclastic eclecticism, his appetite for work, and his hopelessly inefficient yet enormously productive work style.

The man, who more than any other developed Australian political and media studies, had no choice about coming here. Henry arrived in Sydney in September 1940 with 2541 other internees aboard the *Dunera*. The great majority were European Jewish refugees, detained as enemy aliens during a wave of anti-foreign hysteria in wartime Britain. Their terrible voyage lasted two months on an appallingly over-crowded boat, where 'food was scanty; water even more so', and where the troops robbed them and sadistically beat and humiliated them. They spent the next two years imprisoned in camps outside Hay and Tatura.

After the war, Henry studied at Melbourne University. Then from 1950 until he reached the statutory retiring age in 1984, he was a member of the Department of Government at the University of Sydney. Not that he ever retired, of course. Right up until his death in May 1991 he was pursuing with characteristic vigour his usual impossible range of interests.

Henry's career coincided with the growth of political studies in Australia. For a considerable period he was probably Australia's best-known political scientist, thanks to his newspaper columns, his book reviews and his editing activities, in all of which he helped to build the study of Australian politics. It was ironic but invaluable that someone with his background should have been at the centre of this enterprise. His immersion in all the great traditions of European political thought, particularly his critical engagement with Marxism and anarchism, allowed a fruitful insistence on theoretical questions that more insular scholars might have passed over. The historical convulsions which had engulfed his generation allowed a sense of proportion on the mundaneness of the Menzies era.

Politically Henry always viewed liberal democracy as a precious and precarious achievement which shouldn't be sneered at. But he never lapsed into the blandness or complacency that often accompanied such a position, and his intellectual preference was for grappling with strong political positions . . . with wide-ranging ideologies and ambitious theories, often not notable for their tolerance of dissenting views.

In his engagement with the study of Australian politics, Henry was always, as Donald Horne described him, a 'public intellectual'.[1] Through his writings and willingness to participate in debates, he highlighted the principles and dilemmas in political controversies, seeking to influence the shape and tone of public discussion. Equally, for him politics could never be a discipline insulated from the outside world. Its priorities were determined by history, by the influences most drastically affecting people's lives, by the issues which generated the greatest passions.

Henry's most constant intellectual interest was in media studies. This covered two distinct phases, the first going from the early 1950s to the mid-1960s, culminating in the publication of *The Press in Australia*. In the second, from about 1973 right until his death, the whole range of media concerns, from new technologies to genres of broadcasting entertainment, were his central scholarly passion.

What were the uses and gratifications which media studies provided for Henry? One appeal was the media's social centrality. The media played a role 'equivalent to that played by religion in the 15th and 16th centuries' (Curnow and Turner p.14). Media issues in the 1970s were becoming something they had not been before—a centre of diverse scholarly activity and policy movement. 'A situation which seemed almost totally frozen is now getting unfrozen' (Mayer 1974, p.12).

Moreover, 'media arguments, however well disguised, pretty soon turn into some kind of morality play' (Mayer 1976a, p.135).

They pose sharply the most basic concerns of politics: the nature of knowledge, rationality, citizenship, pluralism, policy principles and effectiveness, how institutions work and interact. Thus media provided an engagement with basic values and theoretical issues in a sharply focused and contemporary context, with a stream of fresh political challenges, new scholarship—and plenty of gossip.

Mayer's maxims

What made Henry's contributions so distinctive and what makes his work still so valuable and interesting? From the variety of asides, self-characterisations, the bases of his criticisms of particular works and outlooks, I have compiled the following maxims, which seek to encapsulate his essential outlook. Together they present a unique approach that differentiates Henry's work from all others.

> **There are no cost-free values. The quest even for unarguably desirable values usually carries hidden costs and conflicts with the attainment of other desirable values.**

Central to Henry's political outlook was his insistence on moral complexity, that values conflict with one another, that the pursuit of any value inevitably carries other costs. Recurring themes in Henry's work included exposing the interests behind the philosophy, the mechanical problems involved in the good intentions, the conflicts that arise even among those sharing an ideology, the covert authoritarianism of apparently benign reform proposals.

For Henry, good intentions or apparent ideological virtue were no excuse for lack of intellectual rigour or moral simplicity. I well remember a conference presentation by a visiting American academic on the decline of fairness and balance doctrines in that country. He took these as unarguably good and unproblematic terms, perhaps relying on the presumed sympathies of his audience to allow him to clomp unthinkingly through the epistemological minefield. He stood speechless and uncomprehending as Henry delivered a devastating critique.

No vantage points, or standards of judgment, are absolute or unproblematic.

The standards by which we judge the media or any political action cannot be taken for granted. Partly this maxim is a plea for self-criticism and conceptual precision, but it runs much deeper. So many analyses of media and politics take their normative and epistemological frames of reference for granted. Media performance is weighed against floating normative standards, whose validity is assumed. When critics say the media should do something, the immediate question should always be 'Why?' followed by 'Says who?'

Because the media often serve as whipping boys for all sorts of complaints, the criticisms are frequently characterised by dubious accuracy, and an unwillingness to recognise constraints and achievements. A central theme of *The Press in Australia* was the biases and inadequacies of press critics. The validity of their criticisms was as much a target as the performance of the press itself. In his later works, Henry frequently asked what should and could we expect from the press, from the ABC, from commercial television? How should expectations be affected by the nature of the enterprise, its economics, its organisational constraints, the conflicting interests which make all large endeavours some sort of compromise, and by the links between audience tastes and the normative judgments made. He made similar points about the Broadcasting Tribunal, seeking to enlarge the framework in which critical discussion of its performance occurred.

One necessary consequence is that many of the most common concepts in media analysis are inherently problematic, and need to be constantly subjected to critical scrutiny: balance, bias, quality–popular, left–right, moderate–extreme, independence, accountability. Another is that one's own judgments need to be constantly put into larger contexts, especially to guard against exaggerations made without comparative or historical perspective.

It is instructive to see how Henry applied these same dictums to his own experience. When decades later the injustice of the *Dunera* became a *cause célèbre*, Henry wrote by far the most critical review of the first book to appear:

> Patkin's shoddy work [1980] is not about the *Dunera* experience as a whole. His sole interest is in the minority of *Dunera* Zionists . . . In his narrow focus there is no room for the great variety of internees. The main point—that their hassles were universal (whatever their religion or politics)—is completely missed . . . All this would not be so bad did the work not lack all context. One would think that the *Dunera* was equivalent to a mini-Timor/Kampuchea combined . . . It is even worse to compare our treatment with that of the Jews under Nazism.[2]

He is more generous towards a second book that followed soon after (Pearl 1983). But again he insists on situating precisely the relative degree of suffering and injustice they endured, criticising popular descriptions of the *Dunera* as 'a floating concentration camp'; pointing out how their temporary suffering allowed them to fashion a new life, unlike many of those imprisoned or killed in Europe; and pondering the degrees of wartime injustice suffered by various others, such as the Japanese incarcerated in America, which remain less celebrated. 'To suffer for 59 days is an option many of the permanently deprived of the world would love to have.'

In Australia, there were 'reasonable conditions behind barbed wire' where 'complex and often ridiculous—it reminded me of Weimar just before Hitler—camp structure arose'. He refuses to romanticise his fellow internees, noting for example that when compensation for the shipboard robberies was finally given, many false claims were successfully made. At the same time he notes how the official inquiry whitewashed the behaviour of the offending troops, and criticises the absurd 100 year British ban on key documents relating to the episode.

Similarly, Henry differentiated scrupulously among his oppressors. He is impressed by the time and energy with which the injustice was debated in Britain despite the demands of wartime. He praises the behaviour of the guards at the camp. He praises those from the Society of Friends, some refugee aid groups, clerics and civil libertarians prepared to help, as well as 'Brian Fitzpatrick, Frank Forde and the Transport Unions who all helped to get us out'. He notes that 'non-Labor and Labor governments and military intelligence score very badly' and that the Country Party, RSL and Frank Packer's *Daily Telegraph* were the most bigoted. However, he is more appalled by the failure of those one would expect to act, deploring 'the lack of interest by Jewish organisations' and Dr Evatt.

Partisanship, group solidarity and orthodoxy—any value which places conformity above independence and honesty—are the enemy of intellectual analysis.

Henry's probing exploration of the *Dunera* experience illustrated not only his precision about establishing standards for judgments, but his refusal to allow divisions of virtue and vice, wisdom and folly, to be drawn along group or political lines. The acknowledgment of moral complexity makes him ready to see strengths and weaknesses among a variety of participants. It also implies a critical stance towards the readiness of most people to substitute group conformity for independent thinking.

In Henry's view orthodoxies (and most forms of tribal loyalties) tend to maintain themselves more by creating blinkers and by appeals to partisanship than by intellect. They encourage intellectual mediocrity and lack of questioning. They allow people to mistake the contingent for the necessary, to bury problematic assumptions as if they were facts. The most problematic parts of a political ideology or academic argument are often those to which least attention has been paid.

Political analysts must never allow the contenders' definition of a conflict to become their analytical frame of reference. Their self-images and mutual images need to be subjected to scrutiny. What they take for granted may be more important and problematic than what they contest. The apparent lines of dispute may be quite different from the real bases of contestation; the perceptions of the stakes quite different from any likely consequences. This applies to all political conflicts—between parties, between interest groups and social movements, between countries and ideologies.

Conflict is pervasive and inescapable in all social life. However, particular balances and processes of conflict are the best guarantees for democracy and informed choice.

Conflict was at the centre of all Henry's views of politics. He was 'always delightfully critical of the "harmony boys" ' (Rydon et al, p. 4). However, he did not share the common bias that conflict was, as such, undesirable. Rather the elimination of conflict usually carried undesirable consequences because it betokened the domination of one group by another, and the elimination of choice through the imposition of orthodoxy.

Henry characterised his own view as 'conflict pluralism'. Freedom was diminished by groups achieving monopolies. No interest was immune to the temptations of self-righteousness and expedience. To a media conference in 1975, Henry proclaimed that, given the power and opportunity, we are all threats to freedom of speech. Conversely, even groups with non- or anti-democratic beliefs contribute to democracy insofar as they bring new demands to the political agenda and add to the pluralism of views.

Henry was a connoisseur of schisms. He relished 'theological' disputes among groups sharing an ideology over issues too arcane for outsiders to understand. He also enjoyed splits between people apparently sharing a common vision but based upon clashing ambitions; or how disputes over tactics escalated into accusations of bad faith. For example, his first interest in the work of Gerard Henderson, later to become the most prominent conservative critic of Australian media, came when Henderson's work (1983) disclosed the tensions between B.A. Santamaria and the Roman Catholic hierarchy, a quite different emphasis from all earlier arguments about the Labor Split and the Movement.

Henry had a keen eye for inconsistencies. A favourite example was how within the Marxist tradition, some argued that trade unions and the welfare state prop up capitalism, while others contended that the mass media were unfair to trade unions and the welfare state because of the media's capitalist nature. In other words capitalism caused them to be hostile to what were seen as indispensible props to capitalism.

> **While no views are above critical scrutiny, all views are worth considering even if their style of expression or their conclusions seem outrageous. The validity of an argument has no relationship to its source or to its popular acceptance.**

Many academics profess pluralism; Henry lived it. His range of correspondents and people whose endeavours he encouraged crossed the spectrum. The profusion of publications to which he subscribed not only covered an enormous variety of interests, but sources of every type—academic, industry and professional, mainstream and marginal political groups and assorted social movements. This breadth was, however, informed by an ecumenical scepticism and a pessimism about the quality of all genres. The Mayer dictum of method seemed to be that the means to the limited truth we achieve is through dialectical crap immersion.

This range of reading reflected first his temperament, the thirst for novelty and variety, and second a commitment in principle to pluralism and diversity. Beyond these it also reflected a view of the social role of intellectuals and the political functions of ideas: differences in the power or current social influence of ideas are no guide to their validity or interest. Political groups took up ideas as it suited them. The validity of an argument bore no necessary relationship to its source: Even if Hitler said it, it might be true. Even if everyone in society believed it, it might be false.

Beneath the outrageous expression of views (see, for example, his consideration of the Festival of Light in the chapter on censorship in this volume) are often serious issues that should be examined by those who disagree with them. Because social acceptance has no relation to the intellectual validity of a view, even unpopular views are worthy of serious critical examination. As Kate Harrison pointed out (p. 51), Henry's serious critical attention to media reform groups in Australia in the 1970s and 1980s gave them greater public legitimacy.

Politics is beset by unintended and unwanted consequences. Media effects cannot be inferred from either intentions or content.

The lack of relation between the social setting of ideas and their validity is matched by the ambiguous relation between intentions and effects. Politics is not only morally but causally complex, and Henry's work is within those social science traditions which stress irony and paradox. The consequences of group action or policy decisions are frequently quite different from what their proponents intended (or opponents believed).

Such a view is particularly pertinent to media analysis, where a recurring theme in Henry's work was to criticise those who presumed the impact of any given content or medium on its audience. Commenting in *The Press in Australia* on horror stories in the early tabloid press, which always ended with a moral homily, he asked, 'Who can say how many readers ignored the moral lesson and enjoyed the gruesomeness?' (p. 10). More embracing claims about impact, for example that the media reinforced the system, were easy meat for Henry's critical demolition. He pointed out the problematic generalisations in both key terms, the lack of any demarcation criteria about what would or wouldn't count as 'reinforcement', and the critical confusion between 'support' and 'reinforcement', that one cannot jump from intention or content to effect, without independent and separate evidence (1976c, pp. 134-5).

Henry criticised media reformers and political ideologues whose analyses invented the 'public' that best suited them. He was particularly critical of those ideologies that romanticised the people and their potential while in fact despising them as they are, and dismissing their preferences with theories of hegemony or false consciousness. He was equally distant from those who romanticised popular culture as being the font of great taste or wisdom.

Argument is not a substitute for evidence. Evidence is not a substitute for argument.

Political and media analysis have to be both theoretical and empirical pursuits. The facts about any given situation cannot be deduced from theory, and it takes determined and hard work to produce accurate and authoritative data. Equally, how we describe 'facts', the methods we use to obtain them, the significance and explanatory weight we assign to them, and how they should relate to any given policy proposal or value stance are always problematic, and cannot be derived just from 'evidence'.

Despite his insistence on the relativity of most bases of judgment, Henry's thinking never degenerated into intellectual nihilism. He had a respect for technical mastery, and an admiration for ingenious and painstaking research, especially if it produced new or unexpected findings. But there is also a clear insistence on the limits of science, on what 'scientism' can't achieve, and especially a disdain for giving priority to respected methodological techniques and scholarly safety when it meant ignoring the most pressing problems, or reducing the questions to manageable proportions by ignoring their central or most problematic aspects.

At the heart of his view was an insistence on the irreducible and unique nature of politics, that it necessarily involved choice, clashes of values, competing priorities, and decisions beset by uncertainties about effects. No amount of science could remove the uncertainties and conflict at the core of the enterprise.

To be politically effective you need to form political coalitions with those you don't like. This will also be good for you intellectually.

Henry's strong and sympathetic message to would-be media reformers was that the process of change was typically oblique. Too often, media reformers preferred self-righteousness to effectiveness. They self-indulgently elevated means over ends, preferring to stay within their own milieu, maintaining their subcultural styles and solidarity rather than building more effective coalitions. They presumed that 'if you appealed to idealism that you could not also appeal to self-interest' (1976, p. 224).

Coalition building, thinking seriously about what might be fruitful trade-offs, was not only the path to political effectiveness, but would make such groups and activists intellectually sharper. It would remove their blinkers, take them out of their ghettos of unexamined prejudices to confront their false assumptions and acknowledge other ways of looking at the world.

Making new political connections encouraged one to break through the complacency of established genres of thinking. In the last years of his life Henry was strongly interested in 'green economics', which forced economists beyond their usual political myopia and brought a degree of discipline and 'hardness' that would make green activists more precise and pragmatic. He saw the 'green economics' approach as making green causes more likely to reach fruition in workable policies, transforming them into a part of the political process in a way which would allow more rational weighing of alternatives.

Together these maxims set severe intellectual demands.

They do not necessarily add up to a recipe for consistency. Certainly they are not a formula for complacency or self-satisfaction, for patience and emotional contentment. Nor are they an easy basis for building permanent intellectual cliques and political alliances.

At different times, the approaches were applied more and less fruitfully by Henry. Sometimes the thirst for novelty led to puzzling temporary enthusiasms. Sometimes the iconoclasm seemed to lead to a determined inconclusiveness, a retreat to philosophy when the bulk of the evidence seemed clear. Sometimes the critical faculties were used constructively, at others the result was primarily destructive.

Over time there were distinct shifts in tone. Even though *The Press in Australia* actually endorses several reforms, its general tone is one of downplaying their significance. Yet in his second, much longer period of engagement with media issues there is much more sympathy for reforms, even when some proposals or groups were subjected to withering critiques. What accounts for the shift? What long-term impact, if any, did the passions aroused by Vietnam, the intensity of student protests of the late 1960s, and especially the personal and intellectual explorations brought by feminist challenges have on Henry?

Commitments

How are we to sum up the political and intellectual commitments of which the preceding maxims were part? 'It is silly to ignore what people claim they wish to do, equally daft to take their claims as equivalent to their actual capabilities and effects' (Mayer 1976a, p. 134). Let us apply Henry's advice to exploring his own approach.

Politically he often proclaimed himself a 'conservative anarchist'. True, this was done with a heavy irony, mocking the whole process of labelling and deliberately conjoining two terms most people expected to be in opposition.

Nevertheless, both parts of the label capture an essential element of his outlook. He was ineradicably anti-authoritarian, suspicious of state power and hostile to all social arrangements which denied freedom and choice. He was always looking for institutional arrangements that increased the means for redress, for downward accountability, for increased choice and diversity.

Yet typically conservative themes like the hidden costs of apparently desirable changes and the pervasiveness of unintended consequences of political action also recurred in his writings. He was very sensitive to how the most ambitious manifestoes of freedom could lead to the greatest tyrannies, and how holistic changes often produced authoritarian consequences quite alien to the hopes of their supporters. The anti-authoritarian bedrock of his political ideology combined with what is sometimes labelled a 'realist' view of international relations—that power could only be defeated by equally determined use of counter-power—made him sympathetic to strongly anti-communist policies, at least during the first decades of the Cold War.

Partly, of course, it was that coming from the Europe of Hitler and Stalin, Henry had encountered a larger universe of political possibilities than many Australian activists took seriously. He was especially critical of those on the left who felt that nothing could be worse than the hegemony of suburban Australia.

In public forums and before a variety of lobby groups, Henry frequently proclaimed himself an independent, more self-consciously and insistently as he got older, more interested in the process, in enlarging the scope for choice and rationality than in advancing any one group's interests or demands. He was most interested 'to help improve the quality of public policy debate and to link this with a widening of choices based on knowledge and on genuine alternatives' (1985, p. 1). Similarly,

> I wish to be able to talk to a wide range of interests, often conflicting, without being 'tagged' so as to maximise my life work's goal: to attempt to get interests to fight out their conflicts in a more rational way so as to increase intelligent and self-critical plurality in society and do so with an appeal, not to the intellect alone, but to enlightened self-interest. (Chapter 5)

Henry was pessimistic about the number of people who cared about such things, seeing himself as one of a tiny minority who cared about pluralism and rationality as such, rather than as slogans temporarily embraced to advance one's own cause.

In all his editing and commentary activities he certainly lived according to his creed of 'conflict pluralism'. He focused upon disputes and commentaries, inviting participants to elaborate and confront each other. He acted as multi-partisan cheerleader and arbiter, often as the ringmaster of ideological contestation. Not only did he seek to expose the untested assumptions and evidential flaws on all sides, but to move all combatants from their accustomed battle lines to confront new value dilemmas.

Somewhat analagous to his political self-characterisation as an independent was his intellectual tendency to cast himself as the amateur, the non-specialist. Although he was often very deferential to some experts, or to the need for expertise, this self-assigned role allowed him to intervene on any issue that engaged him. It freed him from the obligations of research, but allowed him to address what he saw as the fundamental questions and the wider significance in any genre of work. In some ways he was in the tradition of European essayists, wide-ranging and strongly interpretative, combining a strong basis in theoretical scholarship with an engagement with contemporary issues.

Henry's primary self-characterisation, so basic as to be easily overlooked, was the primacy of the scholarly commitment:

> For us, critical inquiry is a terminal, not an instrumental, activity. It serves no general 'purposes'. People enquire because they cannot do otherwise and those who do not understand what is meant by this can be given no satisfactory brief explanation. (1967, p. 4)

Appropriately, Curnow and Turner (p. 15) quote Max Weber's 'Scholarship as a Vocation': he could act as though 'the fate of his soul depends upon whether or not he makes the correct conjuncture at this passage of this manuscript'.

In some ways, this is the obverse of being a 'public intellectual'. Here a scholar's priorities are guided by the greatest intellectual challenges, by the most profound questions of theory. The philosophy of law, for example, engaged Henry, because the intellectual pretensions of a claim to be impartially administering justice have an importance beyond whether any individual case may be judged a miscarriage of justice. Fluoridation engaged Henry's attention during the years it was first introduced, not for its instrumental importance, but because it raised questions about the role of the state in citizens' lives, of how to draw the lines between collective responsibilities and individual choice, of the difficulties of rational debate on technically demanding topics, and because of the symbolic stakes so many invested in the decision.

Most importantly in Henry's case, his dedication to the pursuit of scholarship extended beyond his own work, into cultivating the intellectual venture as a whole. In this he was starkly different from the individualist essayists, and we confront yet another irony, the collaborative loner, the individualist committed to promoting the collective enterprise.

Some of Henry's commitment is immediately apparent from the public record, in the huge amount of time he devoted to editing, first for Australasian Political Studies Association (APSA) journals, then for the *Australian Politics* readers, and finally from 1976 to 1991 on the pivotal journal *Media Information Australia.* His commitment to building an Australian intellectual infrastructure was also apparent from his interests in libraries and librarianship, and in the enormous bibliographic project, *A Research Guide to Australian Politics and Cognate Subjects* (ARGAPS 1 and 2).

However, the public record does not show just how much Henry figured in the work of other scholars, the amount of time he spent corresponding and commenting on people's drafts and proposals. Or the way he acted as a one-man clearing house, the tens of thousands of articles he sent to others he felt should see them, keeping everyone in touch with developments. He gave so many people so much help, yet did it all in a way which made it difficult for us to say thank you. Moreover, this energetic commitment to the intellectual endeavour was accompanied by a largely pessimistic evaluation of its products. 'The analytic effort—just thinking seriously—which has gone into the problems of mass media in Australia is laughable, as is the collection of basic information about them' (Mayer 1976c, p. 224).

Perhaps it is fitting that the best epitaph for Henry should come from a leak, and from a comment originally intended as a criticism. Henry's name went before the Fraser Cabinet for an appointment, but he was rejected. Henry later told me that someone, arguing against his nomination, had said, 'he's not one of us—and he's not even one of them'. Then he bellowed with laughter.

Basic Perspectives and Issues

1 Media: Images and Arguments

A generation of students had their first taste of studying Australian politics through the five editions of the Mayer readers, the last three co-edited with Helen Nelson. The first was published in 1966 and the last in 1980. They filled a crucial teaching gap during a period when Australian materials were scarce and not easily accessible, and they had a liveliness and pluralism not always characteristic of introductory texts today.

Henry contributed chapters on the media in each edition of the readers. In the third, he produced stark data on trends towards media oligopoly in Australia, in an article which became the standard reference for all subsequent writers on that topic, even though he personally became increasingly dissatisfied with the implications others drew from it.

In the last edition, Henry contributed two media chapters: one focused on recent trends in Australian media; the other, reproduced here, addressed the dominant approaches in academic work on, and political arguments about, media issues. It dissects the appeals and fallacies of three common approaches—the press baron imagery, the free press framework, and the then new wave of Marxist-influenced consensus studies.

You cannot escape from pollution by holding your nose. There is no refuge from the mass media and their effects. Even if you never touch a paper or switch on TV or radio, most people do all three so often and so frequently that the media affect you through them.

It is very hard to think sensibly about 'media' and society. Few thoughtful people who work in the media–information–communication field and also have some general interest in what makes society and politics tick are reasonably content with what they do and how they do it.

Does it make sense to separate media from society? How, if we do that, can we study the impact of media on society and society on the media? But aren't analytical distinctions essential? Can we say anything general about this which goes beyond a particular social system? Are media under capitalism very different from media in systems claiming to be non-capitalist? How can we decide whether media are mainly reflectors of social processes or whether they affect and shape them? Does this sort of contrast make any sense, in any case? What can we say about the relations of the media to specific sections—women, children, the aged, blacks, businesspeople, scientists, workers, drug addicts, gays, police, criminals? How far should we think of media consumers as basically passive and habituated? Do different media meet different needs and gratifications and do people fairly actively select their consumption to fit in with these? What of the whole process of constructing and then marketing news and entertainment?

It is not that the hard-headed profit-making businesspeople know that what they are after in media 'works'. Certainly not in the sense that they can, except by chance, get whole trends right let alone that they can be pretty sure of what will succeed. The examples of TV series, newspapers and magazines which failed are legion.

Academics for whom media is now a growth industry have tried to impose some kind of order on a very messy field, so messy that there are endless boundary disputes. The most common and most prestigious way is to take some more traditional discipline and 'apply' its ideas and theories to media. A list of perspectives from which media have been and are being studied would include at least economics, history, political and social theory, socio- and psycho-linguistics, semiotics, information theory, psychology, sociology and law. Then, you are likely to delimit the field further and, say, spend your life in looking at pro-social television among a given range of children, till recently likely to be boys. This mode of study and research is still the predominant one and is still tied to the core of the academic career structure. The view of science on which it rests is now under increasing challenge from many directions.

In isolation, and leaving aside the issues of method, such work, at its best, can be impressive. If you look at the comparative work on children, TV and violence which has been a major research focus in those few societies which have a predominantly advertising-dependent commercial TV system (whose existence explains in large part why, in the first instance, there is so much violence to watch on TV), the most appropriate reaction seems a mixture of admiration and depression. As a corpus of work (Murray and Kippax 1978) there is an admirable seriousness and doggedness, and a range of different approaches in which the weaknesses of one are compensated by the strengths of another and the work, as a whole, is mutually supportive. The extent of consensus among top researchers—that positive links between watching violent TV and being aggressive are established—is higher than usual in such fields. The depression takes two main forms: the work illustrates only too graphically what are as yet the limitations of this mode of social science. For those who do not know the long disputes about this, the effort must appear to have a poor cost/benefits ratio. For those who start with fewer expectations it is still disappointing to see how little the vast amount of work feeds back into more general issues about television and society and how very weak it becomes when it comes to policy suggestions. Within its own framework it says very little about what children get out of violence and whether, if it can be approached in terms of uses and gratifications, feasible substitutes can be found. Since violence is itself a concept subject to economic and cultural influences, one wonders under what conditions 'pro-social violence' can be posited and, perhaps, promoted.

Other modes of scholarship are starting to become respectable. There is a growing demand for general advice. Recent broadcasting inquiries and senate committees on children and television and learning had wide terms of reference. Social scientists are now more divided than ever about both methodology and about possible links between thinking and doing. Many are in the double bind of seeing the point of involvement but also having a deflating view of what social scientists have achieved and can achieve. Hence they are concerned that they cannot in good conscience 'deliver' what is expected by those with a different view of the nature and possibilities of social science.

Most discussion of media is specific and segmental. But current attempts to give 'the media' some kind of coherence, a place in Australian society, take three key forms:

1. The press baron image.
2. Applications of the traditional 'freedom of the press concepts'.
3. The media as status quo consensual promoters, which is frequently tied to one of the varieties of Marxism and neo-Marxism.

They exist at many levels of sophistication, they overlap, many people can and do use more than one as they think fit. Hence though what follows is very vague it still imposes much more structure than might seem proper. People use a bit of one angle as a 'mood', another as a 'theory'. It is hardly necessary to say that there is no defence nor intended to be one against the charge that we have the images or their content all wrong or have distorted them.

Barons

The press barons image is apparently fading but you have no trouble encountering it again and again in slightly different guises. Here some basic facts—that we have had and have now some very colourful, highly individualistic and arbitrary media owners who have clearly issued personal directives and became identified with a paper or an empire; that our media and more especially our press is highly oligopolistic, being potentially controlled by a handful of people and firms; that the press at the federal level has been over time overwhelmingly one-sided in identifying its interests and those of 'the nation' with the non-Labor parties—have been parlayed into a very different and much more dramatic imagery. It centres around notions of conspiracy, plots, getting at Labor or at the ABC, giving orders to write this or omit that and doing all this because of 'capitalism'.

The press baron view is now sneered at as too crude and as stressing the role of individuals too much by many on the left who have absorbed a little of more sophisticated Marxist fare. Yet in its many forms it clearly fascinates people. There are endless stories of what Sir Frank Packer or Rupert Murdoch did to powerful individuals and institutions—a prime minister, another proprietor, a top union leader. The imagery is in terms of persons so that the largest media group, the Herald and Weekly Times[1] in Melbourne, gets only the most marginal attention.

The image is one of constant thrust, of deliberate and conscious action. Nothing, so to speak, happens to those people—they make things happen. The stress is overwhelmingly on planning, deliberation or, a major variant, irrational and sudden whims and outbursts.

It is one thing to write in terms of persons and what they do, with but the vaguest reference to any externally constraining factors and to do so because the absence of other material unfortunately necessitates such an approach. It is quite another to imagine not only that you have said a lot but also grasped the essence of and the determinants of a social process and the system it relates to. As people become vaguely aware of the long-run impact of television and as the old barons sell out and fade away, maybe this sort of approach will also fade.

This widespread perspective diverts attention from any serious approach to the study of capitalism and the media. It may well be that in given specific historical periods, media history can be reasonably approached through powerful and striking individuals—Beaverbrook, Syme, Hearst, Luce, Springer, Norton, Reith, Packer, Murdoch. The role of families in an economic system is a proper sphere of exploration. But in Australia the analysis is mostly at the surface and remains there. A good deal of it seems just a cover for ignorance. It blocks work from an essential focus on long-run determinants on the economic, cultural, organisational and occupational aspects of the media. The role of personality will, to be sure, remain a major problem. Deliberate actions occur and can be important, but the way the press baron perspective treats the matter is childish and confined to good and bad, more and less reasonable employers, and getting the right person into a key spot.

The press baron perspective runs a lot like a story in the popular press. It has drama, but mostly pseudo-drama. It has 'human interest': what Rupert said to Gough; who is dining with Mal at the Lodge. Its focus is mainly on proprietors but where this is hard you can change the status of the barons and make them editors. It is a spotlight view in which particular people pop up and then vanish—there is no desire to work out what they might share as a type, what their roles are. People who would blush if they told history in terms of kings are apparently unaware of what they do when they talk of media institutions and empires.

The image of the barons and oligopolists can be stated in many ways. A sophisticated one is to relate the small number to the economic and social background, to link people and instruments of control:

> The incestuous nature of the interlocking companies and directorships provides this small clique of proprietors with perhaps the most effective grip on the instruments of a national media that could be witnessed in any part of the world . . . What also makes the situation frightening is that most of the proprietors who operate these groups share a common social background and in political terms share a common point of view. (Keating 1976)

Yet the linkages and interlocking ownership and control do not have much force as such: they are, to be sure, often mentioned but mostly in abstract and general terms—very rarely when it comes to the ownership and control of television and radio. There, the mention is obligatory but almost entirely ritualistic: there are few stories of what the great baron did with TV or radio. People do not often link the effects of what worries them about television with barons or with ownership: the link, if any, is with transnationals, cheap US imports and directly with profits. You don't hear about the 'barons and sexism'—here it is 'TV' as an impersonal widespread process linked much more to the system of broadcasting than to people. Thus 'barons' don't come into the content or alleged effects of the most important medium—television.

It may be that a proper analysis of this kind is justifiable in historiographic or sociological terms. Until this is shown the approach through powerful and mostly nefarious (but possibly valiant) individuals can only be used as a temporary and very superficial sketch/story. In Australia a lot of media work and media discussion has got stuck there.

Free press framework

The traditional freedom of the press view has usually worked at two levels: At the first, the press should be free from governmental controls and from the intervention of any external standard-setting bodies and forces. It should set its own standards of accuracy, fairness and equity. It is, within the law, accountable only to its readers. The accountability consists in the unchallenged but negative right of readers to stop buying the paper. If they have any other ways of holding the paper accountable those ways and the extent to which they operate are decided by the paper. It alone determines the way in which it will maintain the standards of integrity, responsibility, fairness, accuracy and so on it subscribes to.

In a very interesting letter in which Sir Warwick Fairfax explained why his firm refused to join the Australian Press Council (Gunaratne 1977) this view is put clearly and ably. It is a view which rests on total confidence in one's own reputation and integrity as earned through long work. Put this way it means that you can speak, logically, only for your own firm or for firms whom you recognise as having the same standards. But if you do that and proclaim judgment over them they can claim to do the same to you. Sir Warwick, quite consistently, says the Council would not be

> of any assistance to firms such as ours which have gained a reputation for maintaining a high standard of responsibility to the public in 144 years. We do not think it would have any appreciable effect on newspapers which aimed at different standards. It is not our function to sit in judgment on other newspapers and we would strongly resent their sitting in judgment on us.

Such a view cannot be criticised if one accepts its foundations for it assumes the paper is isolated, and it assumes that a tradition of service to a given clientele exempts the service given from any external checks. The service is evidenced by sales.

It is not possible to state, let alone defend, such a view consistently. If you link it to sales then you cannot very well have only a one-way link: the *Sydney Morning Herald (SMH)* would not argue (and would be silly if it argued) that its long-term decline in sales shows that it has become less responsible.

But the paper would not assume that sales validate and legitimise the integrity of products it did not approve of independently. None of us makes such a judgment as a matter of course: if we disapprove of heroin and sales go up over a long time we say that (a) people's standards or resistance have deplorably declined and/or (b) that they have been pushed and misled by some malevolent force into supporting heroin and will be sorry for it. People who think the *SMH* is part of 'capitalist dope' would find increased sales among workers evidence for nought but a more subtle and hence more nefarious form of hegemony. They would deplore and 'expose' this new instance of 'false consciousness'.

The *SMH* over the years constantly defends not just itself but all those press competitors over which in this context it won't sit in judgment. It cannot, within Sir Warwick's framework, give any reason why it should be the sole judge of its own integrity except to repeat that its integrity is beyond challenge and that it, and it alone, must judge standards and their modes of enforcement. So all the *Sydney Morning Herald* can and does say is that it believes it tries to practise integrity by its own standards and that it also believes it has succeeded. That it has those two beliefs, and holds them as part of a long tradition, and with moral commitment, is true. It is important in appraising the paper. But that does not tell us anything about the nature of the standards themselves. Nor does it give any hint of a reason why a firm belief in its own virtues should entitle it to be its own judge and jury, to assert that it alone should determine both the norms and whether they have been broken. That is, in fact, the claim made.

The second, and much more common, defence of the freedom of the press concept indirectly admits what the first one denies: that this freedom is itself to be thought of in utilitarian terms—the factual reporting and investigative and fairness functions of the press entitle it to the very minimum of controls. But they are linked to the minimal information required to permit the electorate, as citizens, to form some kind of rational judgment not only of policies but also of options among them.

Who is to judge whether the job has been done? At what level? With how wide a choice? What do citizens 'need' in terms of minimal information in a democracy? Clearly you open up a mare's nest so that, for instance, if you think there is an intimate link between being capable of reasonable political judgment and material of a certain kind about parliament you will then think the press has a 'duty' to have lots of such material. If you are sure that the vital areas of rationality and choice are in the Christian–humanist, uranium, tariff or Asian field your priorities will be very different.

Once you talk, even faintly, of responsibility of media, the issue of who should judge what the standards are and whether they have been met cannot be avoided. The main fear of the Australian press—in Europe many countries have major press subsidy schemes which, initially, have produced none of the predicted horrors (Smith 1977)—is that it might become dependent on government or be controlled by government (Wiltshire and Stokes 1977b). It has defined 'subsidies' so that special postal and telecommunication rates do not count as such. In doing so it is no different from, say, academics who don't think of themselves as paid for by the government. 'The community' or 'the public' sounds ever so much better.

Where governments have to state functions or objectives, as in commercial broadcasting, there is the difference that they deal with people who are not supposed to be owners of the spectrum but only licensees. Hence they have 'obligations' in return for the use of a national resource. In principle this enables governments to impose any conditions they favour as a condition of the licence. The licensee can decide at which point costs outweigh benefits. To the licensee any conditions other than those which are narrowly technical and tit-for-tat (interference and technical matters) are too burdensome and constitute 'government interference'. Reformers wish to invoke the power of government to impose additional conditions. In Australia, the commercial TV stations resist not only rules which would lose them money or prevent them increasing their profits but also some which might help them to make money. They favour the thin-end-of-the-wedge argument and take it seriously. In the United States over-the-air broadcasters spent decades lobbying their Federal Communications Council (FCC) regulators to screw down the competitive cable TV industry and prevent broadcasting investments. During those years the cable interest did not fail to point out the inconsistency. But when optical fibres via telephony started posing a threat to cable who, do you think, ran to the FCC regulators and asked them to check the nefarious new growth? Locally, commercial radio has been more hostile to regulation even than TV. But they quickly sought government action for the prevention and, failing that, the slowest possible growth, of public broadcasting.

Given that you must put down objectives for broadcasting, intelligent public servants will do precisely what they have done, with considerable verve and skill in recent reports. They will prefer to give a very long list, with lots of very broad objectives. These will and must be peppered with the indispensable terms 'adequate', or 'undue' (Postal and Telecommunications Department 1976, pp. 25–41). You can later get rather less vague and link specific sectors with specific tasks. Necessarily those allocated to the most important and politically influential sector, commercial broadcasting, must again be very general. The exercise is not silly nor unimportant. The words have an important symbolic and ideological function. They can and will be used in public to try to extract at least moral responsibility from a broadcaster—commercial, public, or national. Terms such as 'adequate and comprehensive' in legislation serve as flags round which to mobilise sets of interests. The standards cannot normally be unidimensional, easily measurable and objective, like the proportion of an hour in which you can advertise. Most are bound to be 'vague', but they still have politically and socially important functions.

Any reasonably long list will be full of contradictions. That's in the nature of the enterprise. Only if you have to summarise your symbols in one paragraph do the inevitable incoherencies in this type of operation emerge—and then only if you read it with great care. Few people do. The currently fashionable portmanteau ideal nicely combines variegated vistas reaching upwards and outwards in multiple directions with a reminder about external constraints:

> The [Australian Broadcasting] Tribunal believes that a broadcasting system ought to reflect and encourage a diversity of life styles, ideas, attitudes and value systems. It ought to reflect the widest possible range of variety, information and opinion. It should be flexible, diverse, editorially independent and accountable to the public. It should seek to enrich the lives and widen the horizons

of the people it serves and it should also reflect the environment in which it operates. (Australian Broadcasting Tribunal 1977, p. 6)

What if a major diverse current is that which is deeply suspicious of diversity of life styles, and which sees in 'enriched' lives the seeds of decay and disaster?

The 'freedom of the press' arguments in relation to the role of the Australian press seem to have very low priority and little general support in society. There are no specific data, but in one poll when asked to rank issues in terms of priorities only 4 per cent put 'protecting freedom of speech' first. The survey as a whole confirms the impression that concern for issues of this kind is related to both higher education and youth, with a significant proportion of the young and tertiary educated interested in 'democratic' and civil liberties issues. But they are atypical (*Age*, 12 and 13 June 1978).

The minority who care about the adversary and investigative functions of the press would not believe that the press as a whole displays them. One of the main difficulties of the old freedom of the press argument is that by any set of reasonable, conventional criteria only a small minority of papers tries regularly to meet them. On the most charitable judgment all you could say about the vast majority is that they still have some reporting functions.

There is outside its own ranks only very limited support for 'freedom of the press' notions: few people believe that their freedoms are in some ways bound up with that of the press. You can easily test this by talking to any cross section about specific powers to suppress specific things, or see how they feel on such issues as libel laws restraining investigation. The feeling that freedom of the press is in some sense bound up with readers' interests can be generated if they feel the paper is a trier and is honest within its limits with 'accuracy' being taken for granted. 'Accuracy' alone does not lead to active support as such. In order for the press to get solid public support, it needs a constant *display* of news and features of what your readers can see as honestly trying investigative journalism.

Papers which have standing with their readers and with politicians, papers with weight and all the old virtues have this quality. To a different extent and with different parameters this is also true of some public affairs programs on TV. The *Age*, the *National Times*, the *Australian Financial Review* all have this aura. What is expected is a sense of trying, a sense of making it now and then, a sense that the paper cares, a sense that it is not always partisan in supporting one side through thick and thin regardless of merit and issue, a sense that it will take risks, a sense that the journalists and the editors will 'have a go', and that they will be aware of, resentful of, and fight against restraints.

The lack of support for freedom of the press arguments comes partly because the bulk of readers, viewers and listeners have not the faintest notion of what an impossible job under incredible conditions good journalists in both print and broadcasting are confronted with day by day. The main reason why they don't know is that the media don't choose to tell them day by day what an impossible, fragile, crazy enterprise the whole concept of a daily paper or show on deadline is with the product you have routinised and processed and finally put out being originally unstable and partly unpredictable in origins, location and content. Ombudsmen, ombudswomen and readers' representatives and, to a lesser extent, media critics are a fairly obvious way of institutionalising this. They can work and are in no sense 'radical' let alone 'anti-capitalist'.

The media, and more especially the *Australian* and Rupert Murdoch were involved in a major way in the 1975 election with an important strike by Murdoch's journalists. There were accusations of 'news fabrication' and counter charges by Murdoch that they had 'cut bias out of' journalists' biased stories. Among publishers and newspapers only Ranald McDonald and the *Age* publicly responded with any sympathy for the critics. Ranald McDonald stated that 'Our credibility is at an all-time low'. Further he opined that the ALP had not had 'a fair go' in the pre-election period, that the 'media fell down in not providing enough variety in news and opinion' and they had not been 'effective' in querying Malcolm Fraser's vague program (*Journalist* April 1976). The *Age* editorialised:

> The duty of the Press is to expose, not oppose. It is to seek truth, not to wield power; to be vigilant, not politically ambitious; to criticise, not overthrow. It is to discover the news as diligently and dispassionately as it can and to publish it as quickly, fairly and accurately as possible. And in politics the function of a news-

> paper is, we think, clear: to report politics, not to play them; to report and comment on politics without political motivation. (16 March 1976)

Developments at the *Age* and elsewhere within what was once taken as the most stodgy and hidebound newspaper firm in Australia, John Fairfax, suggest that we should look again at the various dimensions of media oligopoly in Australia. Under what external constraints can editorial 'strength' manifest itself and how far can it change the constraints? What is the role of market forces as against ownership in influencing content? What is the relation of oligopoly to hegemony? Our provisional inclination is to be increasingly convinced not only that the dimensions of oligopoly in the media field at least are much more complex than was once thought and its relation to potential and actual control much more loose than is widely believed but, more importantly, the whole issue of ownership and content needs a fresh look.

All these papers remain pro-capitalist. For those for whom this is the sole or main criterion everything else, by definition, must be superficial and peripheral. In a slightly more sophisticated version: a more subtle and devious way of reinforcing hegemony by tokenistic changes. For others who are interested in changes within the system and are willing to use different criteria of significance, the study of the factors making for change and the limits of such change is now more urgent.

Nor need the violently anti-Marxist despair: they too can use differentiation within the same ownership empires to show they have always been right. There is a long line of work in America, not in the mainstream but plentiful, which uses a press baron in reverse approach. It makes the decision makers (who are conceived of as really running the show in spite of formally powerful but actually powerless owners) the journalists or broadcasters—especially left liberals in network TV news. In the extreme version you get John Birch society pamphlets (sold here by the League of Rights):

> Conservatives know that the Communist Conspiracy has thrived only because its real nature and accomplishments have been hidden from the American people by those who dominate the mass media. The Establishment Press provides a paper curtain behind which Communists and Fabians have operated in America

> for many years . . . The mass media in America whether it be the newspapers . . . network television, or the slick magazines, are disproportionately in the hands of the radicals of the Establishment. (Allen 1970, pp. 1, 32)

The American versions ran from important analysis about the relative liberalism of TV, consonant with 'traditions' stemming from Marx or Schumpeter as to the halo-undermining and self-destructive tendencies of capitalism or with Weber's 'rationality', to the worst kind of sewage about the Jewish conspiracy in which Carnegie, Rockefeller, CBS and, especially, the *New York Times* all figure.

Christians are surely right in 'positing a secular-humanist hegemony in the mass media' (Muggeridge 1977). In Australia, for many years *News Weekly* and B.A. Santamaria have, fairly specifically about sections of the ABC but much more vaguely about the press, suggested some kind of de facto workers' control by journalists of media in which the journalists impose a left or leftish line on the powerless or 'soft' owners. Their conceptualisation is hopeless, their 'evidence' wafer-thin, yet if the issue is posed less ideologically it is worth pursuing.

Consensus and Marxism

The late 1960s and 1970s saw a major development in media and communication studies. Many people were convinced that media were much more central to society and its modes of legitimation and reproduction than had been realised and that the earlier methods of approach were inadequate. In a large number of special fields—media and development; communications and world society; media, culture, class and power; media and ideology or hegemony; media production, processing and organisation—old orthodoxies vanished. By 1978 what suspiciously looked like new ones had become fashionable.

A few very loose ideas had become widely accepted but they were very broad indeed. In Australia there are few strict theorists in any field relating to communication and media studies. Typically, many people have picked up some general notions and use them as they see fit and do not worry much about what they should call themselves or what they are called by others. The general mood was predominantly 'left'.

1. *Constructionism.* Most lecturers taught that news was an artifice, that it was made, fashioned, shaped, manufactured, produced, constituted, constructed and reconstructed. The elements going into and accounting for the artificial product from sources to organisational and economic determinants to camera angles to newswork conventions were discussed at length. Marxists could use this sort of approach by talking about events being processed into newsworthy commodities.

Just what followed from constructionism was more contentious: were there any universals across history and culture and economies? If so what were they? Could one make anything into news so that people would look at it and attend to it? But if not, then was one back to implicitly sorting out some events as inherently newsbearing, lodes of news with 'mine me' on them? What difference did constructionism make to journalism? How did it relate to TV? How did it affect the news vs entertainment distinction?

2. *Skew.* 'Bias' in the sense of conscious and deliberate slanting away from some objective norm was fighting a losing battle as a concept. Were there many planned actions in the news? Did you need a concept of objective truth which constructionism seemed to have undermined to talk that way? Ritual and habitual repetition of taken for granted professional and technical work practices, of organisational patterns never seen as contentious leading to definite skew, was the more fashionable notion. The scope for accusations of skew was endless—towards or against the establishment, ethnocentrism, the ruling class, the patriarchal society, the class system, racism, agism, uranium mining.

3. *Patterned skew.* Most people had some vague notion that what was skewed and in what direction it was skewed was not accidental nor nicely pluralistic so that what you lost on the swings you made up on the roundabouts. They believed and taught that skew was linked to power, status, class, the elite, the rich, the top dogs, the ruling class. Some were beginning to link skew with 'the authorities', including civil servants and linked in various ways with secrecy, databanks, ASIO and restrictions on civil liberties.

Notions of labelling, of blaming the victim, of making the poor or the unemployed or the young into 'problems', were becoming more common. Similar trends could be found in work on the professions, on welfare and social work in which the notion of the system being structured so that the professionals would keep control at the expense of and for the alleged benefit of 'the clients' of the system were widespread. It was touching to see the professionals making careers out of a critique of the professional careerism of others.

4. *Status quo legitimation.* The media were increasingly seen as constructing reality in such a patterned and skewed way that they reinforced, perpetuated, reproduced the existing ideas and structure of the status quo. They legitimised it. They spread ideology that it was the most natural, the best, the most beneficial system. Challenges to the status quo were, in the crudest of media, simply chopped out or never considered. The media determined the framework (agenda) within which people could think about public affairs. They determined priorities within that agenda. The more subtle media had 101 methods for dealing with challenges which they had admitted or had to admit: burying them, labelling them, using pejorative language, cartoons, comics and photos, running them for a short while only, not supplying context, making the enterprise seem irrational, utopian, idealistic, absurd, subversive, impractical and not worth taking seriously, putting it down as the ideas of stirrers, perverts, deviants, crazies, militants (who had heard of militant employers?), reds and terrorists.

Little work had yet been done on how it was possible to get past these barriers and traps and what new difficulties lurked in the field of 'alternative' or 'counter-hegemonic' media.

People, of course, differed a lot as to how bad the status quo was, who were its key beneficiaries, how long it might last and how it might be changed or overthrown. They differed drastically about the role of and the definition of 'economics', 'politics', 'culture', 'personality'. Increasingly some of them tried to 'bring in' sexuality and the family.

Outside the newspapers themselves, it is hard to think of anyone who either defended the old notions of press and media functions or publicly criticised strongly the new ones. There was little in the way of the most obvious questions. What was this system being compared with? How far would one expect media to be autonomous and critical in any society? Were they more critical here than in other societies which were also capitalist? If so, how could one ascribe their features here to a system as such rather than to a specific historical variant (or was it a deformation?) of it? Why, insofar as media supported the status quo, was this considered rotten without further discussion? What did these views say to those who did not find the evils self-evident, or who found other systems worse, or who saw in the system's critics only the ruling class of tomorrow? Just what could be done about the media short of a total change? How far was the view that media were change-preventers and consensus-reinforcers a semantic one in which 'change' was so defined that by definition nothing that altered within the system was 'real change'?

As for concepts of patterned skew and putting down: How far was it true that media also constantly put down some top dogs? If one compares media images of doctors, lawyers, academics, civil servants or scientists with that of workers or blacks or women, how far would one find similarities of treatment? What should one say of the media habits in left and trade union journals? How defensible was a view which implied that, by definition, all differences between newspapers were marginal and uninteresting? How much did the whole enterprise presuppose that there was a science of society in the sense that one could equate support for the system with its legitimation and its reproduction? If you did not accept the notion of a 'system' in the way it was put forward, what became of the whole enterprise? Only a very few adopted such views in a way which forced them to draw uncomfortable consequences from them. They preferred not to push things too far, to be inconsistent but committed to some minor reform.

None of the general images of the media are well worked out. However, while the field is now much more messy than it was a few years ago, there is some evidence of new questions and an air of hope. It would be nice if it lasted—alas, the new shots in the arm are already producing many adverse reactions.

2 Control, Accountability, Influence

This paper was presented at a forum at Murdoch University, in which the two principal speakers were Henry and Ranald McDonald, then Managing Director of David Syme (publishers of the Age*). The terms for the forum address three central issues in media theory. Henry's preparation for the paper was careful and extensive, no doubt partly due to his respect for Ranald McDonald. Elsewhere he had written:*

> [*The*]Age *in Melbourne is Australia's best paper. Ranald McDonald has for some years taken, in public, a position which is very different from that of other top executives in the media and is not approved by most of them. Ranald McDonald . . . is the only person in his position to talk about the press in Australia in an intelligent way. What he says is seldom startling as such and in no way 'radical' but in the Australian newspaper context it is very startling and very radical . . [He is the only publisher to have recognised] that all is far from well, that the press has a major problem . . . a crisis of confidence and credibility.*

In this and other chapters written before the advent of the Hawke government in 1983, it is important to recall that Labor had only been in power for three of the previous 33 years, and that they still had some pretensions towards adopting policies of major reform in media. This is one of three previously unpublished papers in the current selection.

Control

Control of the media is the issue which has most preoccupied Australian media critics. They are obsessed with the goings on of press barons, with bias in the news and with oligopolistic control by three major groups. The facts are not in great doubt. The amount of concentration in Australian media is unparallelled in western society.

The objection to concentration has nothing to do with whether you are a Labor or Liberal voter, or whether you are independent. It is common to every type of democratic theory I know of. The objections are that the criteria for news selection and news presentation are arguable, and that news formulations can and do vary. Given those two undeniable facts, it is intolerable in principle that criteria for news presentation and news selection should be in the hands of so few people. On the assumption that news presentation and news selection are forms of power, it presents a form of concentration of power in society unchecked by any institutional balance, which is unparallelled in a democracy. There is no institutional diversity, and there are no institutional checks and balances to the news formula. That has nothing whatsoever to do with whether the papers are pro-Labor or anti-Labor, whether they are lousy or excellent. The objection is one of principle, namely the principle of so much potential and actual power being in the hands of so few people. Those people are not elected and are not directly responsible, but they have the power to decide what issues should receive prominence and how they should be presented. Given the additional power connected with the cross ownership of television and top magazines, the case becomes much worse.

The above is the standard case put forward by everybody who lectures in media. It is theoretically perfect, but totally irrelevant to Australian society. In fact, the objection to oligopoly in Australia is a phony and dishonest one that has been kept alive mainly by academic critics, and has no value at all for the actual study of media in Australian society.

Australian media probably offer more diversity than most Australians want. If all media were owned by one group, and there was one independent paper which presented a highbrow version for people like myself, most Australians would be happy. They would not know who owned it and they would not care about the content. As to how many people own media—two surveys have shown that most people don't know and couldn't care less. The economic, social, cultural and psychological basis for any kind of pluralistic or diverse society, or demand for diversified papers in the abstract, does not exist. Australians are not interested in abstract points about democratic theory. People think about diversity and ownership only when a particular person, in recent years Mr Murdoch, 'treads on their corns'. Only then do they get annoyed about the general principle of oligopoly. Nobody on the left denounced Murdoch as an oligopolist when he supported Labor in 1972. He was denounced only when he switched against the ALP. The point is that the arbitrary power is the same in each case, whether you approve or disapprove of the purposes for which it is used. The ownership point is quite abstract—most people know nothing about democratic theory. Hence the ownership issue is not a live issue in Australian society.

Once we distinguish between formal ownership, carrying with it the right of potential control, and how often and under what circumstances that control is exercised, the simple picture of Australian media control, as the clear expression of a single policy by each of the big three (Herald and Weekly Times, News/Murdoch, and John Fairfax) becomes much more complex.

Leave aside on this occasion legal issues—what proportion of what kind of shares with what sort of voting rights constitute 'control' and how far 'control' is defined differently by (say) the Trade Practices Commission, the Australian Broadcasting Tribunal and the Stock Exchange. Ignore complexities about the composition of boards.

Even if we all agree on what formal control was (and there is not much agreement once the lawyers get into the act) there are two distinct issues: What is the de jure structure of formal control? and: What is the de facto pattern of control as exercised?

These two aspects are related 'in principle' but at a high level of abstraction. True, if you have formal control or hence the right of control you may exercise it 'when the chips are down'. But when and how often are the chips down? By itself this is a statement only about a possible crisis whose likelihood we do not know. It could be a statement which is related to self-censorship: a paper may behave so as to make as sure as it can that the chips are not thrown down. However, this is a counterfactual statement. It is very rare that we can do much with it. 'Self-censorship' so as to anticipate trouble surely exists—but when you have said this there is not much to add. What we want to know is the normal behaviour of a newspaper in relation to its formal controller. Here the concept of formal control by itself is pretty empty. It cannot tell us on what range of issues and under what circumstances the *Brisbane Courier-Mail* is de facto marginally or fully independent of the Herald and Weekly Times.

The fact that a paper is owned by a group is not necessarily helpful even for making policy predictions within that group, as various experiences among the Fairfax papers have shown. Nor does knowledge of formal control help predict when or if particular publications will be subjected to what controls by the company.

When the Murdoch/Melbourne *Herald*/Fairfax battle was on in 1979, there was great fear of a Murdoch win. But that fear existed: (a) because it was thought that it would lead to further concentration; (b) because of Murdoch's reputation as an interventionist who imposes uniformity and is a ruthless employer; and (c) because most of the people who feared (a) and (b) also did not admire and often detested his standards of journalism. If the *Age* were to take over (to be absurd) the Melbourne *Herald* how many people would really worry about a thinning in the number of papers or about the Fairfaxes indirectly having extended formal control?

The issue of concentration of control in the print media and that of cross-ownership is not inherently tied to the particular concerns of the ALP. Control over the number of broadcasting stations which any one firm can own or effectively control was introduced by the conservative Lyons government in 1935. The relevant minister, Archdale Parkhill, was a highly conservative man. Yet he said in December 1935: 'We have growing up in this country a monopoly of newspapers and broadcasting which, in combination, constitute a danger that this Parliament cannot view with equanimity, and steps should be taken to deal with it'. And his government, in 1935, was the first to limit the number of stations one firm might own. True, it eased the specific regulations after an intensive lobby. The cross-ownership issue did not come up partly because the federal government has no constitutional powers over print media.

The ALP's record on the print media control issue is thin. It has never had a major plan to seriously tackle print oligopoly indirectly, nor to set up a corporation to help minority papers. Labor's policy on broadcasting is a relatively comprehensive one, but that is not true of its print media policy. The ALP should be at the frontiers of exploration of new possibilities in media. It ought to pay major attention to how new technology can be used for genuine pluralism. Instead, it is mesmerised by oligopoly and its main efforts have been spent in mild attempts at counterweights or the checking of broadcasting media power. Given its assumptions, this is fine. But the effort is pretty negative and there is not much exploration by Labor of new possibilities created by changing technology. (New ideas, whether about public broadcasting or new community TV, have not, mostly, come from party people.)

How far the ALP really feels (as distinct from making speeches) that the press treats it very badly and that but for that it might be much closer to power is not known. If its actual efforts to overcome those barriers are looked at one must conclude that either it does not take them half as seriously as it claims to or that it has given up all hope of overcoming them, or a bit of both.

It is not proper to criticise the Liberal Party for not being a party of media reform. They have used the oligopoly through an increasingly successful setting of the media state, especially in the electronic media, and better control over the timing of strategic leaks. Labor, of course, also manipulates media whenever it is in power at state level.

I must conclude that control per se is, regrettably, not a real issue. Mr McDonald has stated that it is related to credibility—concentration of control means loss of credibility for the press. This surely holds for his paper, the *Age*, and maybe one or two others. But I cannot believe—much as I would like to—that it holds for the bulk of the print media. (When Mr McDonald speaks of the press in general terms he cannot help but cast the mantle of achievement over others, often unworthy of it. This comment is not critical of him but a description of the structure within which he has to work. But one always needs to probe what Mr McDonald is defending when he talks of 'the press'.)

The truth is, alas, that plurality and diversity of control of the print media has no firm cultural, historical or institutional basis in Australia. In my more gloomy moments I think that for most Australians there may be too much diversity in the media, too many conflicting views even within one paper, that they find even the very limited range of variety that exists a burden. If this is so, it does not help to play around with the ether-like concept of 'hegemony' which, after a promising start, has become an obstacle to serious inquiry.

Media control in the hands of the few then becomes a more general issue when something the few do control becomes an issue. The specific event is linked, for ritualistic purposes, with oligopoly. In Australia this is helped by Murdoch being ideal for sticking pins into. The concentration of control issue is purely a civic goody-goody issue which is dragged up at election time. It shows the impotence of the ALP and the impotence of people to deal with the media. Feelings of unease about oligopoly in the print media are diffused, low level, and not tied to any plan of action. It is not a force which governments normally have to consider.

Accountability

Much of the discussion on broadcasting policy and, increasingly, on telecommunications policy is linked with notions of accountability. There is not just one can of worms, but many. All that seems clear is that there is nothing even vaguely resembling a unidimensional and internally coherent concept of 'accountability in broadcasting'. Moreover, the formal role of 'the public' varies a good deal: 'the public' has no institutionalised specific role in relation to the ABC except for a few on futile advisory committees. Its general role is as electors—and this raises major questions as to how far and in what sense the minister responsible is 'accountable' to 'electors'.

The public can be *given* special roles in submissions to, and providing inputs at hearings of, the Dix Committee of Review. But the key point is that the opportunity to be able to show public capabilities and public inputs is entirely at the discretion of the government. There is nothing corresponding to the initiative in Switzerland and some American states which enables a given number of electors to compel the authorities to put an issue on the agenda for public participation (or even public decision making through referenda).

Secondly, in broadcasting, given the existence of a federal power to control, given a long tradition of ministerial activity, given formal control (at least) by some body with quasi-judicial functions, given the existence of licences which have de jure and de facto open and indirect conditions attached to them, given above all some notion that the public has rights (whatever that means), there is widespread use of the concept of accountability as a major taken-for-granted part of decision making.

As soon as one gets down to specifics the grand concept of public 'rights' becomes attenuated and hedged around with so many conditions and qualifications, and the exercise of these attenuated rights becomes so hard, that there is a temptation to say that 'nothing' remains. Recent important work by Mark Armstrong (1980) and Kate Harrison (1980) shows that this is an oversimplified view. If one had to oversimplify in one or two words, the dispute would be between 'very little remains' and 'nothing remains'. However, both papers are written from an angle which takes the existing right to regulate for granted and attaches little importance to 'self-regulation'. A scholarly anti-regulation, pro free enterprise, pro self-regulation paper—not hard to find in the USA—does not yet exist here. It might discover too many public rights unduly burdening industry where Armstrong and Harrison see few. And this shows the importance of taken-for-granted concepts however messy, multi-dimensional, inchoate, porous, contextually restricted they may be.

The first key question which must be asked is: 'How far can, as a matter of fact, legal rights held in some sense be exercised in a given institutional setting?' The answer is usually depressing for the advocates of public and participatory rights. But it is superficial and misleading to leave analysis there without also asking a second question: 'What have been the social, psychological, self-image, economic, institutional effects on the structure or interests involved of the very existence of and display of the concept of "accountability"?' The most ambitious attempt would be to then relate the legal–formal–administrative level to the extra-legal, socio-cultural level.

Newspapers

Whatever the legal rights of the public vis-a-vis commercial, national, public and ethnic broadcasters may be, it has none in relation to newspapers insofar as their news values and news practices are concerned. The public has specific rights in relation to advertising and as customers. There are rights related to defamation and, possibly, to privacy.

However, any 'rights' which are mentioned as 'citizens' and are related to the process of news definition, selection and presentation cannot be legal rights enforceable against press proprietors or journalists. The conventional view of 'freedom of the press' as being, at the least, freedom from government legislation in any way related to news content means and must mean the absence of legally enforceable rights in this area by citizens. For such would involve governmental legislation. That is why the Australian Law Reform Commission's proposal for a legal right of correction in defamation is symbolically so important, whatever its efficacy might be.

There is nothing unusual about this. The formally most important civic right relates to voting. Yet there is normally no way in which citizens singly or in organised form can assert any rights they might have in relation to electoral systems, malapportionment (gerrymander), or redistribution policies. Governments decide what the scope and power of Courts of Disputed Returns shall be. After that and by that act legal rights as defined exist. Most things citizens may feel worked up about, whether about elections or about newspapers, are not justiciable—you cannot get them into the courts, and you have no standing.

Newspapers are accountable to or responsive to their readers only to the extent that their owners and editors decide that they should be. This, to be sure, is a statement that would not satisfy those press editorialists who, when challenged as to accountability, vaguely refer to consumers' sovereignty through market forces. It is true that whatever might be meant by 'accountability' or, usually a rather weaker term, 'responsiveness', the market element enters into the second concept in terms of survival and of having to exist by selling the presumed attention of their readers, stratified by demographics, to advertisers.

The relation between the market and the paper is very slack. There is a large number of things a paper with a clear identity, such as the *Age* or the *Sydney Morning Herald*, could do which would be (un)desirable from some other point of view but would make no difference to circulation, type of reader or advertising.

One of the main results of media research is that mass communicators have but the vaguest concept of what their audiences are. In spite of ratings, this is also true of TV and radio. Only a detailed study could discover what determines judgments by decision makers as to how far and in what ways they ought to be 'accountable' and to whom. One may assume that it hardly ever will be an abstract commitment to the moral rights of citizens. Yet, since 'good business' may go hand in hand with 'social responsibility', even that is not a safe statement. Judgments will be prudential and will be derived from the interpretation of 'responsibilities of the press', of 'journalistic traditions', and (especially in the David Syme and John Fairfax case) 'traditions of the firm/family'. They will take into account perceptions of what readers want, what they will put up with without stopping to buy the paper. They will consider what kind of trouble organised readers tied to interest groups can make, and what image advertisers will get.

The key themes of socially responsible, rational capitalists like Ranald McDonald are much the same as democratic theory: that participation in decision making processes makes the participants more reasonable and teaches them, through practice, how to exercise and expand reason. It forges closer links between those affected by decisions and decision makers, so the decisions embody greater elements of common sense, are less oppressive. They do not have to be imposed with as much coercion as otherwise they might have to be.

Participatory practice thus closes the gap between them and us. Of the many difficulties in this conception two are centrally relevant here: it is not clear how this sketch of action is supposed to work if one assumes serious conflicts (class conflicts would be one instance) between 'them' and 'us'. One then either has to assume that rationality over time modifies and minimises conflicts of interest or these are seen as so crucial that all we can have, short of a total break, is manipulative pseudo-participation in which the lower groups are made to feel they have a chance to change things and have changed them when they have not done so. Nor is it clear who is to distinguish, and on what grounds, between 'genuine' and 'fake' participation. (The concept of ideological ruling class penetration of all social consciousness (hegemony) as linked to an essentialist idea of class conflict means that for those who subscribe to both most participation is manipulated, a form of 'repressive participation'.)

Mr McDonald's general argument is that a newspaper which explains itself to its readers, responds actively to their preferences, helps them to organise their needs, identifies its concerns with theirs, must strengthen itself as a paper. It will be more alive, it will be more responsive, it will be more flexible. Because it opens some of its secret cupboards and admits at times that it is fallible, because it is less self-righteous than most other papers, it builds up trust and credibility.

Fortunately Western and Hughes (1983) in 1979 repeated a 1966 survey. The comparison suggests that the public perceived most media as being less fair in 1979 than in 1966. The sharpest shift towards perceptions of unfairness was for the press—towards both the coalition and the ALP. We do not know what part 'fairness to parties' plays within a more embracing concept of credibility, but it seems reasonable to guess that there has been a sharp decline in the perception of press credibility over the 1966–79 period. We do not know how this relates to a particular paper, such as the *Age*, but it seems clear that Mr McDonald's concern with declining credibility touches on a real and serious problem.

Credibility is central to this concept of a paper's relation to its readers. Credibility is linked with authoritativeness on political and social matters and hence with the weight the paper carries: the paper is seen as capable of mobilising, if need be, a goodly proportion of its readers. Credibility in this sense is also a valued and valuable commercial property: in a quality paper advertisers can feel that some of its credibility as a newspaper rubs off on their advertisements. Such papers are often crusading and investigating 'excesses' of capitalism and they tend to check and control 'disreputable' advertisements.

Quality papers thus see it as part of building up their credibility to foster a 'clean' social system. They, like the *Age*, are good at digging up land scandals, corruption in the public service, shady deals and violence in trade unions, illegitimate behaviour by civil servants or by the police. The investigative and probing part of the paper not only builds its credibility but also reflects its conception of 'accountability'. If it takes the watchdog role seriously this in turn shows that the paper is fearless, that it works at digging out the truth, that it 'takes on' the government or other authorities and calls them to account in the name of its readers.

People who consider the capitalist system inherently exploitative and oppressive will see the 'excesses' as merely the most visible expression of all round rottenness. They will see the attempt to clean them up as necessarily futile (another pustule must break out) and as diverting people from the need for radical social change. The investigative role cannot touch the centre and cannot even remotely impinge on ruling class interests.

Given a view of capitalism which leads to the demand for its overthrow and which posits a ruling class, the press cannot be 'accountable' to the ruled, since the same model posits a zero-sum conflict between rulers and ruled: the power of one can increase only at the expense of a reduction in the power of the other. The press, in this view, is a major institution which legitimises the capitalist system and its class rule and which in a number of complex ways helps it to survive, adapt to pressures from below, and shores it up so that it will continue ('reproduction'). It sees accountability as a classless concept which must be rejected: whatever Mr McDonald's deepest convictions and his and the paper's intentions, they cannot but help 'in the final analysis', being 'accountable' to the ruling class whose instrument they in fact are.

Since this is clearly a pretty crude view, recent neo-Marxist work has introduced a great number of complexities: ruling classes are seen as coalitions so that some conflict (but not on 'basics') between and within class fractions are part of the notion of ruling class. Sectors of the system, including the press, are seen as having 'relative autonomy' and there are complex theories of segmentation. There are many competing Marxist views of the state—the main differences revolving around the concept of the state as the simple instrument of the ruling class and that of the state as having relative autonomy from sections of the ruling class and enforcing the longer run interests of the ruling class and the system as a whole. This mode of analysis can yield, in intelligent and trained hands, a good deal of flexibility since its dogmatic and metaphysical 'foundations' can play but a ritualistic role.

Responsiveness, openness

The idea of accountability is linked for a paper such as the *Age* with its response to what it takes to be readers' needs and demands. Its main effort has been to allow restricted entry to parts of its fortress. It has, for example, pursued a policy of announcing tie-ups with enterprises David Syme owns which gives the *Age* a self-interest in managing news about them or may be seen as giving it such an interest.

While the *Age* remains entirely the private property of the owners and controllers it has decided that it is both good business and good journalism to let its readers have a 'go'. The paper has been opened to them by more space in letters to the editor; more direct access to the paper by a telephone brief views service which makes contact rapid and easy; and the use of editorial page space for views opposed to those of the paper or in some way 'different'. It has not yet gone for the notion of a newspaper ombudsman (not yet 'ombudsperson') which seems to have worked rather well on some US papers and been a flop on others.

In its attitude towards its readers and its practice of being comparatively open and responsive, the stance taken by the *Age* is not unreasonable. Given the paper's leading role, its commercial prosperity and its resources, it is now also reasonable to ask it to be yet more innovative and bolder.

What sort of image of its readers can one infer from what the paper does for and with them? It assumes an up-market middle class, relatively well-educated readership. The readers make sporadic and quarter-hearted attempts to be 'decent' provided decency does not involve any permanent and serious efforts. Even more often, they feel they ought to be rather more sensitive and unhappy, feel mildly puzzled and guilty that they are not, and then donate more generously than usual to the next appeal or buy an extra land rights button. It is a readership that, overwhelmingly, does not link its occasional unhappiness with any issues of major structural change. Mostly it finds talk of 'capitalism' and 'socialism' boring, puzzling, abstract and irrelevant. It is basically satisfied with a social system from which most of it, given their goals in life, benefits. Up to now it does not see clouds as seriously affecting its own comforts. The *Age* readers do not like open displays of racism or of sexism. In other words, like most of us, the readership is neither heroic nor saintly nor 'committed' (you will call it 'fanatic' if you do not like the given commitment).

The public perception of where the *Age* fits in the left–right media spectrum supports the characterisation of the readers and the paper as mildly left of centre (Horan, Wheeler and Lenehan 1979). The stress is on 'mildly' and a reminder is needed that in Australia the centre is such that what is conservative in many European countries is 'left' here.

However, this all-round characterisation is misleading as the final word, since it takes no account of the many subgroups the paper caters for. The *Age* has a good deal of variety and one of its major strengths, which gives it guts and a feel of being non-plastic, is that it gives space to non-progressive views in a deliberate manner. The range of diversity is, to be sure, limited. The paper is poor in looking at the best of English and American neo-conservative thought. It is very poor in its news from countries which claim to be socialist (it's better on features). At the same time, the treatment of China is unduly uncritical. It does not do enough in trying to get different news sources. It tends to prefer another good US service to one from Scandinavia or Southeast Asia.

If one looks at both news and features, an *Age* reader over a year or two gets a pretty good and wide range overall. In quite specific areas I think the paper is poor—my first example would be the reporting of UNESCO's attempts to do something about a 'new information order'. It featured major attacks with no real attempt to summarise UNESCO's admittedly jargonistic, verbose yet often valuable material, nor to give a process-oriented background which extracts and highlights its legitimate complaints.

To summarise, 'accountability' has been practised by the paper in many informal but important ways: by opening it up to its readers, by being a bit more open and a bit less self-righteous about 'the press', by some probing of new demands and needs and, above all, by a constant incremental attempt to bring out a better paper and conform to its own standards of what that should be. These are all worthwhile things. It should be clear that I believe that the *Age* is 'a good thing' and that its attempts at responsiveness are not mere tokenism. It does not concern me much that one cannot really distinguish between 'responsiveness' and 'accountability' here and in this context I have not made any attempt to do so.

Yet uneasiness and serious doubts remain. Too much depends on the drive and on the ideas of Mr McDonald, and the accidental fact that he is where he has power to act. The paper and the company have total discretion in deciding what the process of responsiveness shall be, what its limits are to be, how speedy it is to be, and towards which specific publics the paper is to be open.

There is a genuine dilemma here. If we find an institution which is being run in ways which make you feel hopeful, which keeps on trying to do better and which also listens to outsiders, it seems mean and ungrateful to ask it to institutionalise a process which depends too much on a few personalities. Yet one would like such issues looked at and settled by some process going beyond self-criticism. It may well be that it is not desirable nor possible to regularise the process of response, to give it an institutional base. Moreover, it is clear that to institutionalise a process does not, in itself, guarantee much. If I were to guess which is more responsive to its 'clients', the *Age* or the ABC, the *Age* would win. If I were to make the contrast between the *Age* and licences being in some way 'publicly accountable' to and via the Australian Broadcasting Tribunal, the *Age* would also win. Hence only a dogmatist would claim that to institutionalise an informal process in and by itself is a guarantee that public rights of a moral or legal kind play a larger part in decision making than if the process is left to hang loose.

The trouble is that few papers are like the *Age*. One looks for more formal processes where newspapers are unresponsive or meet serious and concerned criticism by patronising recitation of the fact that no one compels you to buy that particular paper and by a ritualistic reference to 'freedom of the press'. The more unresponsive and self-righteously indifferent to growing concern papers are, the weaker will be their public support against any serious challenge from governments, unions or rival owners.

Limited types of complaint can be fixed by the Australian Press Council most often in its informal role. But there is nowhere one can discuss general news values and news selection policies—it is precisely those which are under greatest challenge—and have an assumption that the decision makers are at least listening.

How is one to compel press responsiveness if not given? How can one raise issues of public concern with the press and go beyond its self-defined scope of response? Many of the heavy suggestions for complex bureaucracies won't work. But the questions remain real, permanent and central. It is in the long run (but not, to be sure, in the short run) self-interest of the press to work out an answer, together with its well-intentioned critics.

How one judges the totality of these attempts in the abstract depends on the standards against which one appraises them. In relation to other Australian dailies they add to a considerable effort in a field where it is easiest to do nothing. They work fairly well given the sort of readership the paper has and the usual irony applies: for those who by virtue of social position, education and family training have already a good chance of being aware of their rights, and are able to assert these, the *Age* offers yet more of the same sort of power. It may be that its practices of responsiveness and openness unintentionally widen the gap between the information rich and information poor. But that is not the whole story. One would also like to know what spin-offs from this process come to others. How far do the middle class paper and middle class concepts influence and spill over into other strata? How far do they act as 'role models' for some of the poor and the unorganised?

Self-criticism in the 1980s is no longer so hard. It would, if practised, in time increase support for a good paper which makes many defensible decisions, the rationale of which is not known to outsiders. Overall, it is time for the better papers to move forward. They could work towards a much better knowledge of readers' potentials; they could try out alternative news formulae in parts of the paper over a long time so that options would be easily available. They could think of ways of explaining more fully what they are after and practise some of that famous inventive journalism on themselves. They could go for highly visible reforms which are genuine but also have major symbolic value.

Given its history and the assumptions about government intervention, so deep-seated that they cannot be easily overcome, there is no way in which the Australian press can be made formally accountable to its specific readers, its workers, or to 'the public'. It is not necessary for our media industries to make much of an effort yet since their critics are not well organised, are highly segmented, are often sloppy in their well meaning work and cannot get their act together. They are, for the most part, strong on moral indignation, but not much else. Indignation is a necessary but not sufficient requisite for reform activity.

Influence

The major source fashioning 'the public imagination' for the bulk of the population lies in the messages of the mass media. These direct daily attention to what are to be, as a result of that attention, the persons in the public eye and the public issues of the day. Personalities, causes, parties, movements and problems one is supposed to know about cover a broad spectrum in the media. It is in and through the media that they emerge, exist as 'public', and fade.

Being in the media's, and thus the public's, eye is so central since Australian society pays lip service, at least, to the duty to know about 'public issues'. A good deal of the socialisation process is concerned with this. To be indifferent is to be 'apathetic', a pejorative term always used with an implication that it is a state to be overcome. To refuse to know is a sign of low status and narrow and selfish vision. The way the Aussie slob image with pot belly, beer can and 'she'll be right' attitude is used is typical. 'She'll be right' is not merely a display of indifference to action but also of indifference to the issues and problems one is supposed to know about and in relation to which one should act once knowledge of them is gained.

The large proportion of people who feel deep hatred towards and disgust with all public issues find it easy to be 'indifferent' but much harder to express their contempt publicly. It is hard to get publicity for a total rejection of the duty to know, to care, to be involved.

The ideology of disclosure as being healthy for democracy is widely shared across classes and strata. Few apply it to their own affairs: businesspeople who want unions laid bare do not feel the same about the affairs of business and vice versa. Most academics who want newspapers to reveal their processes are less keen when they are asked to publicly explain the inner workings of university selection committees. There are a few people who consistently fight for a general freedom of information and for an all-round information policy.

Critics of the press want more disclosure of what they take to be the forces and institutions on which the press depends: it is a sign of autonomy. Hence the standard question as to why the *Age* does not investigate as much of big business as it does of government, small business and local councils.

The attack on secrets, the high value of openness and its link with enlightenment is used by all and sundry: sex shops do not sell 'adult products' merely to make money but to help stamp out furtiveness about sexuality. *Penthouse* and *Playboy* mix exposure of the body with that of the mind. A broad range of issues and activities can be 'linked' with the need to know, the glories of diverse choice, progress and democracy. This argument can be mounted for picking the right party to vote for and making a choice of wallpaper for the home. There is a very important case against disclosure made by Burke. But the case here is made by civil servants. There are complex ties between this obligation to know and, much more selectively, to care, and the ideology of citizenship and of democracy.

It is not merely a question of most people not being able to experience most events and processes outside their personal ken except second hand and vicariously. That must be true of any fairly complex society open to outside influences. It is rather that this is so and that our ideology fosters (lip service to) awareness and awareness of public issues that is so important. The media stand for making one aware. Most clearly this awareness/enlightenment role emerges in papers such as the *Age*. It stands for investigation and what it displays in spite of obstacles corresponds to a widely held view of knowledge the public interest requires.

All mass media are linked to public issues but the link is most obvious in daily newspapers. In their daily work they construct the very public issues they write about and then report on and must allocate priorities between them. They must decide whether X rather than Y qualifies as an 'issue'. Once it does, they must decide whether to give it more or less play than some other 'issue' and they cannot avoid decisions of that kind even if they have not been discussed or planned beforehand but initially emerge from practice. Media must constantly construct agendas to which people attend. Even if they set out to deliberately renounce all influence they could not do so: they take part and must take part in the major processes by which attention is allocated. Hence they must exert an important influence.

Most of the inevitable sorting and ranking is such that there is no conceivable way in which media could normally act as passive reflectors or 'mirrors'. They are rarely mere 'messengers', simple conduits for a message for which 'reality' or 'the world' is responsible. For a daily capital city paper to be mainly 'a mirror' there would have to be: (a) consensus on what is to count as an event or process; (b) consensus on what are the criteria to separate all newsworthy events from all non-newsworthy events; (c) an equal degree of attention to the initial observation of all newsworthy events and an equality of resources needed for their transmission with no cost differentials; (d) an automatic and mechanical compression/selection process which adjusted the newsworthy supply to space.

Nothing comes even roughly close to these conditions, even in totalitarian societies. Experts can and do study their papers for clues revealing lack of mechanistic uniformity. Condition (d) cannot even be stated without begging the question by writing 'newsworthy events' instead of 'events'.

Hence by the 'ordinary' process of selection and given the fact that there is always a set of other events that could have been selected, that there are always alternative modes of display, newspapers are inherently an artefact and news must be that too.

That news is an artefact which is fashioned, defined, created, decided on, manufactured, and transformed from a very large (if not infinite) number of occurrences is a platitude for media analysts. None of them believes that newsworthiness inheres in events. Part of their job is to explain why many journalists react with uneasiness and hostility to this idea. What is implied for the analysis of media influence by their omnipresence as suppliers of artificially constructed vicarious accounts and experiences?

The most common way of studying media influence is to separate, conceptually at least, a world of non-media events, attitudes, actions and structures and then look at media as having influence on them, effects on them and of course vice versa. Then we can ask specific questions about 'influence'. The most favoured has been the influence of media on election results. Political analysts focus on elections because they are frequent and regular; because they have gone on for a long time and hence one can construct time series; because the results can be expressed in quantitative and fairly simple terms and because they are supposedly linked with 'issues' which in turn are linked with reason. It is comparatively easy to get funds for media research related to election studies. Committees have heard of them and think that if so many people do them they must be important or, if not important, at least 'safe'.

The typical study looks at the media's record in news presentation in a specific election. In Australia—this is not so common overseas—it is very likely to start from some assumed model of 'reality' which if it were 'reflected' by the media would represent 'lack of bias'. It then most likely tries to chart how the paper or the TV news presented the ALP on given issues. It then, in spite of assurances to the contrary which it might contain, is most likely to infer that whatever is known as to media content and 'bias' has some links with the outcome of the election. The sophistication of the basic design varies: increasingly, more recent studies may engage in a flirtation with 'meaning' by some use of semiotics and some implied notion of how the news is 'read'.

But in a world in which the media's influence must willy nilly penetrate into all major aspects of the symbolic environment and cannot be separated from it even analytically, this sort of study and approach is less and less justifiable. The assumptions—that one can look at a long range communicative process this way; that there is a relation between content and perception and cognition by audiences which is non-contextual and can be read from the content alone; that if you show 'no effects' you also show the absence of media 'influence'; that after analytical separation of 'media influences' from other factors it is then possible to put the media factors back into a total picture—are all highly contestable.

Agenda-setting

Early media work was influenced by the fear of radio as the great manipulator and also concerned with 'propaganda'. It looked for 'scientific proofs' of the dramatic effects of media and did not find them. It was followed by a long period of work, often in itself perceptive, which ended in 'disappointment'. The search had been for media impacts and effects which changed things. Instead the media seemed merely to crystallise behaviour and reinforce attitudes and behaviour—'the law of minimal consequences'.

Leave aside all issues of 'methodology'. Assume that in fact the work of those years showed what it purported to. What is striking is surely the conceptualisation. These were years in which it was assumed that people would obey governments. There was no special interest in or puzzle about the continuation of capitalism. Because the ideology behind the question—change is good and fascinating and worth reporting, reinforcement is dull and not a 'consequence'—was of the crudest progressivist kind and had no concept of habit and continuity as problematic, the 'findings' were labelled as 'disappointing'.

From today's possible perspectives they are not so. If you approve of the system you will be cheered to hear that it is being stabilised and reinforced against possible challenges. If you think the system is rotten, exploitative and oppressive then what is being reinforced ('legitimated') and continued ('reproduced') is infamous. The role of the media in the process is a major and vital function.

'Reinforcement' is not disappointing given an assumption of problems of ungovernability/legitimation. However, it seemed so for most researchers. They thrashed around for a while till agenda-setting entered the scene. The key proposition of agenda-setting research is that the media may not tell you what to think but can and do tell you what to think about. This seems hardly a stunning discovery since the early speculative work of Walter Lippmann on the relations of news to liberty, on problems of the press and on public opinion clearly contains that view. But Lippmann was not a 'social scientist'. He cannot be found in the index of most US texts which also fail to mention Jacques Ellul, Jurgen Habermas, Antonio Gramsci, or semiotics.

The excitement agenda-setting caused is not hard to explain. Given that one was to show 'effects' of any interest you had to try and discover a new 'finding' which would save the existing methodology and help to perpetuate positivism as the dominant mode. The agenda-setting researchers, most particularly Maxwell McCombs, seemed to have the way out of what was seen as a deadlock. In terms of existing methodology they could show 'effects' which were tied to political cognition, especially perceptions of issue salience. The terrible 'law of minimal consequences' seemed overcome.

Agenda-setting is a very hot property. Its key proposition is that the media pay greater or less attention to a set of issues and that those exposed to the media will adjust their perceptions of the importance of issues in line with the agenda in the media. Hence the way in which media select and list and give space to 'items' and themes exerts a crucial influence on the agenda of public priorities. To know the prevailing dominant media agenda enables you to predict 'public opinion' as to the salience (importance) of given issues. The causality runs from the media to the public agenda.

Speculations

Even if these hunches sound convincing that does not make them right. Hard slogging has to be done. A variety of methods are needed, amongst which open-ended surveys will play a part.

1. It is likely that the media are much less powerful in setting the agendas of people at the top and at the bottom. People in the elite have many extra-media sources and a broader range of personal experience of 'public issues'. They also have easy access to a range of non-Australian media whose agenda might conflict with the local ones. Conversely, if you have opted out of the system or have been labelled by its processes as on 'the outer', mainstream agendas must, if 'out' means much, be less important for you.

2. Federal and state agendas are likely to differ. How does the convoluted mix between national and state structures affect agenda-setting? Is the state-centredness of papers in the less populous states affected by their ownership by Sydney and Melbourne oligopolies? How far is there an Eastern states agenda and how far is it split between Melbourne and Sydney? [An] innovative paper by Jim Walmsley (1980) put forward the notion of 'spatial bias' in the media in a very convincing way. Does this over time influence rural perceptions and if so whose?

3. How is agenda-setting, whatever it may be, seen by dominant elites and to what extent do they adapt their policies to their pictures of an agenda they cannot get on to? Politicians, even those who think the press is biased against them, do not believe that it is better to be out of the biased media than at their mercy. During a major journalists' strike in 1980, the Labor Party decided not to give its press releases to the management staff working the papers, a stance Bill Hayden commented was hurting them politically.

How far do politicians, for instance, seriously consider press and TV aspects in advance of policy making? Is it true that for Labor, the press and the perception it has of the press agenda works as a major excuse and scapegoat? Is it true that when the party bombs out, to 'curse the press' is one way out from a serious self-examination of what is 'wrong'? (Note that such an examination most likely would blow the party to pieces. The Labor image of the capitalist press may well be one of the necessities for the party sticking together in an unthinking way, muting the standard conflicts and rarely getting into office.)

4. What are the relative agendas of press, radio and TV? In

broadcasting, how far are there conflicting agenda in commercial, national, public and multicultural broadcasting spheres? What will be the effect of possible audience fragmentation through cable and electronic publishing on the notion of a common media agenda?

We have said enough to suggest that the main issues lie with how elites—senior public servants and business and union leaders—see the influence of the media, how far they take it into account and in what ways.

It is very likely that media agendas must be linked to class and stratification aspects, including those of information needs and knowledge. In the US agenda research has not been tied to power and class agenda differentials but has been of the most naive kind, with many consensus assumptions built into it.

In Australia non-Marxists and Marxists have rarely been able to work together. But neo-Marxists now operate with class fractions. This should enable them to try and tie different agendas to these fractions. For them, of course, the fraction would cause the differentiation in the agendas. But that may only be 'in the last analysis'. There is room for 'relative autonomy' and a long way before the 'last analysis' will separate honest, serious and hard working researchers.

The influence of the media, then, is not so much in electing or bringing down governments, but rather in fashioning the total image of a given society. It is in that way that the press is absolutely vital. The general framework of society is formed overwhelmingly by news people. The usual context in which these problems are discussed—usually in terms of bias and partisanship, pro- and anti-Labor and oligopoly—is not very fruitful.

Conclusion

Given rising costs, hassles with unions, deadlines, insufficient space and resources, every measure that seems clear cut and simple to the outsider turns out to be more complicated and has to overcome more obstacles than one imagined. Those obstacles may come from journalists and other workers. It is unjustified to present management as reactionary and stupid and journalists as progressive and flexible. It is just as unreasonable to reverse this image.

Australian media reformers have all too often tended to be the worst enemies of reform. They are not sufficiently self-disciplined and have not taken sufficient trouble to understand the problems of the industry. It is not being suggested that if they did so it would make them less critical—it might make them more so. But reformers' ideas have a better chance if they are based on solid homework.

We know very little about Australian media. None of the methods of analysis are very powerful or convincing. There is nothing in a way of overarching theory. Nor will the endless reiteration of the need for one bring it closer. It behoves us to be humble, to be self-critical of our own assumptions, to tie media studies to our general picture of the social structure, to be sceptical about any interest claiming to embody truth and virtue—including our own interest. We must combine imagination and intellectual honesty of the most uncompromising kind and grub in the dreariest of facts and get them right, not just nearly right.

3 Media Diversity Reconsidered

Diversity and pluralism were for Henry fundamental issues in any consideration of the media. In 1981 he presented two papers on media diversity and its bases, one to the Australian Communication Association (ACA) conference, the other at the Australasian Political Studies Association (APSA) conference. The APSA paper is more tightly argued but the ACA paper more stimulating, touching upon many more ideas and issues. The latter, somewhat tamed and with a few important inserts from the APSA paper, is given here.

The tone of the paper is pessimistic, showing Henry's conviction that most people cared little about such issues in principle, being only concerned with getting a better go for their particular point of view. Although diversity was widely used as a slogan in political debates about media, he felt that few had considered with any rigour how it could be institutionalised.

> I think it would be a pity if I grew any bigger in Australia. There are now basically three groups in Australia and that's too few already. If I were to grow bigger and take over one of the other groups—or be taken over—that would be against the public interest. I'd like there to be six groups. The fewer there are the worse it is. (Rupert Murdoch, 1977)

> We believe that in the interests of objective reporting of news the widest possible spread of ownership of the media is desirable. (The platform of the Liberal Party of Australia)

> It is notorious that 95 per cent of newspaper proprietors have long since surrendered control of editorial policy and news content to their journalists who enjoy complete autonomy unless and

> until they run the ship onto the financial rocks. (*News Weekly* 22 July 1981)

In a long and increasingly complex tradition, one of the main ways in which we can distinguish between more or less democratic structures is by looking at the degree of media diversity. Diversity here refers vaguely to both the number and content of media. It is seen as tied to choices. Given assumptions, explicit or implicit, as to competition and freedom, choices are in turn related to democracy.

This is the simplest and most popular way of making linkages. Most theorists use much more complex ways. They look for linkages between choice and knowledge and then try to establish some notion of knowledgeable choice as linked to democracy. Or they will go on, in the currently fashionable manner, to inquire into the conditions for 'genuine' choice and into concepts of choice itself. In such inquiries passivity is tied to ignorance and activity to knowledge and, in the longer run, rational choice. The interests which a mere passive consumption of media products are said to serve are charted and criticised. The idea of an active media public is put forward. Activity is taken as selectivity, as a major aspect of a more critical public mind. Many plans for 'access' to and 'democratisation' of media are then tied to this conceptualisation.

Here it suffices to note that the notions of an active public or ideas of an extended public sphere and of more participation are linked with choice amongst diversities. This is so because the tacit assumption is that of a distinctive range of publics engaged in conflicts or struggles. There is little agreement as to what concepts should be used to analyse, let alone possibly forward, such struggles.

It is widely assumed that diversity of media content is linked in general ways to a wide spread of ownership in the case of newspapers and to autonomy and internal freedom in the case of statutory corporations such as the ABC. But is it true that autonomy and anti-proprietoral or anti-managerial trends and pluralism of ownership are related to diversity of media messages?

This paper argues that there are no necessary links between autonomy and diversity in the ABC, and that news people nearer to the bottom of the enterprise are not necessarily tied to greater critical diversity. We speculate on the homogeneity from the top vs diversity from the bottom theme for TV, publishers, magazines, the SBS and journalists. Is there something interesting in the extreme right crackpot comments about journalists being on the left and running the paper? There is.

The traditional argument linking diversity and spread of ownership has a power strand, an occupation choice/autonomy strand, and owner-content strand. In any specific case all the old arguments may, indeed, hold. But you cannot link this with any theoretical concepts or patterns. Equally, in any given case: (a) formally separate owners can and do have major links; (b) formally commonly owned papers can and do compete; (c) formally differently owned papers which compete can be very similar in content; or (d) owners may run papers in similar or different ways in terms of policy and market segmentation. How far can they fashion markets and market gaps?

Very depressing conclusions follow. Not only can you say little about 'diversity' in general, but you cannot predict how owners will behave. Hence you cannot tell who you might have to back at a given time in the name of a better chance of content diversity.

Bias

For decades three major themes have dominated work on the role of the mass media and communications policy in Australia: bias; diversity; and ownership and control. 'Bias' has moved with increasing momentum from an uncritical two-sided (mostly Liberal/Labor) balance concept to structural inbuilt skews against particular sections (women; Aborigines; ethnic groups; non-Christian religions; gays). Within the relatively larger groupings, the structured skew type of argument can continue towards solipsistic regress: lesbians may rebel at treatment by male homosexuals in gay media; transvestites may feel there's gay media 'bias' against them. Currently we are urged to consider the liberating kindness of misunderstood S&M and bondage supporters.

But note that complaints about media 'bias' are just as rife amongst top dogs, 'exploiters' and 'oppressors'. If you find a group, section, fraction, faction, elite, or class, set or network which does not claim that the media bucket it and are biased against it, just move a little. Australian complaints about media bias about trade unions can be partly paralleled by the US literature which treats the 'capitalist' press as 'left', undermining business authority and American society.

None of these allegations about bias are inherently unimportant or meaningless, though many specific instances are such without a theoretical context. The issue is linked with traditional notions of press exposure, investigation, muck-raking, digging, and watch-dogging. The task is to link these with conflictual and skewed structures of particular interests and ways of living and then, maybe, to fit that into overall structures. There is no difficulty in saying that media simultaneously legitimise and delegitimise.

It is easy to expand 'bias' notions so that they re-emerge as agenda-setting, legitimation, hegemony, and (cultural) reproduction ideas. Concepts of this sort are the most fashionable, porous, and stretchable. They can be easily 'linked' (that is, mentioned in the same breath without worries about weight or causality) with narrower and more specific instances of skew. I am aware that 'skew' is relational and highly contestable.

Diversity

'Diversity' is related in complex ways to 'bias'. In some contexts they may markedly overlap. People who almost ritually use the term seldom think of power, control, interest, or domination. Most of them might have a low interest in politics. Perhaps they are less likely to be macro and holistic thinkers. Compared with talk of bias, supporting 'diversity' is less likely to lead to bipolar imagery: It gets you close to the type of multiculturalism defined in terms of non-menacing food, ceremonies and dances. Thus you can rehash the form of 'pluralism' which links with tolerance, consensus and co-operation.

Absences of 'diversity' need not be conceived of as structurally related: You can harmlessly multiply diversities you believe are absent. They appear as desirable colour flecks in a basically sound skein. Their absence is to be regretted, but the wool is not rotten. We can add, given goodwill and finger pointing, colour flecks at will. This is the 'Year-of ...' diversity approach where you pop in a UN designated group. It yields very similar articles about the media's bias against women, the child, the disabled, the aged. There is a vague assumption that such sectors are linked by being 'deprived'.

The key points are hardly even raised: How are the various sets linked? Why do power holders or high status occupations—doctors, lawyers, public servants, businesspeople, scientists—also encounter media 'bias'? Assuming the answers would yield major complex linkages, if the only choice allowed was between 'nothing but' separate fragments and 'nothing but' patriarchy, homophobia, class domination, or ageism, you have no option but to go under protest for the second alternative, and then fight at once against its absurd simplifications.

Ownership and control

The ownership–control theme has many variants. All have symbolic and dramaturgical possibilities, in which personalities are crucial and institutions become anthropomorphised. Feminists might ponder why we end up with Granny and Aunty.[1]

Conceptions about media diversity underlie many discussions about the ABC. The institution, insofar as it is 'independent', is seen as a guardian of diversity. Within the ABC the creative staff is seen as the guardian of independence as against the politically stacked Commission[2] and against management.

In general, the view is that there is a positive correlation between the ABC's 'independence' and programs or actions which are 'diverse' and 'different'. The greater the independence, the more clear cut the boldness of different hues, and the more of an alternative will the ABC be. Much less worked out, yet a theme of long standing, is the notion that within the ABC 'the Commission' and 'management' stand for blandness and not offending the status quo, while producers and 'creative staff' stand for some kind of guts, enterprise, verve, stirring and boat-rocking which can be described as making a contribution to alternative modes and to 'diversity'.

But it is not true that the 'independence' of the ABC is necessarily tied to its offering alternatives or diversities. You can find cases where diversity was imposed by governmental fiat on the ABC. The ABC's independent news service is by now sacred. At times some people have seen it as a major alternative to the news from the commercial press and as a purer, better, and more detached alternative to it. Without looking in detail at the service and its reputation, the decisive point here is that in the 1940s it was established against an alliance of ABC Commissioners and the Chairman and all major press proprietors except Ezra Norton. It was imposed on the ABC by a Labor government linked with a dissenter within the ABC, Frank Dixon, who for years had struggled for a service. He was severely victimised by the ABC afterwards, but the independent news service has, for long, been part of a tradition for which the ABC, of course, now takes credit. Of course, Labor had no concern with diversity as such; it hoped, in vain, to make the news service its tool and wished to counteract a hostile press.

In 1975 two new and different radio stations were set up by the ABC—3ZZ in Melbourne and 2JJ in Sydney. Clement Semmler, who did not like what the stations do, saw this as yet another instance of 'truckling to politicians'. He wrote of the 'shame' of the ABC accepting 'what was tantamount to political direction without demur' (Semmler 1981, p. 33). For us, two questions: Was the ABC de facto directed to set up the stations?—Yes. Were these stations seen as very 'different', as adding a dimension of 'diversity'?—Again, yes.

For us the relationships between autonomy and diversity, hierarchy and diversity, and ownership and diversity are problematic. In a given case you might, for instance, have to back a less autonomous media body against a more autonomous one because you guess that overall diversity will now be increased. Mindless ABC 'friends' automatically supported Aunty over the Fraser government's creation of SBS since they argued (correctly) that SBS had much less autonomy. But it also has a bureaucratic interest in product differentiation, that is, diversity of a multicultural kind. This remains the case whatever its structure, its programs, its relations to ethnic communities. One may argue that the diversity it has an interest in promoting is fake, minor, too bland, too WASP, establishment tied, not sufficiently political, nor related to the 'interests' of ethnic groups. If one argues thus, one is evaluating types of diversity and making a division into those which matter and those which do not.

When people interested in such issues talk informally, they make two main points about ownership and control, dependence and autonomy. One is linked to some notion of human, moral and legal rights as such, without too much reference to whether they are being exercised and what effects such an exercise might have in a given context. The other tacitly refers to rights but puts the main emphasis on assumed improvement in the product or area of enterprise to which their exercise specifically refers. For print media, especially newspapers, the stress is on product, then rights. For licensed broadcasting media the emphasis is on rights as such before the consequences of their exercise.

For newspapers, goodness-from-the-bottom is assumed. It is taken for granted that if the owner does not push round the editor and does not 'interfere' with him (rarely yet 'her'), the paper will be better in the sense that it will be closer to the traditional free press watchdog notion. Owners are thought of as oppressors in the name of corporate and self-interest, editors much less so. When it comes to notions of reporters' power in various versions of workers' participation (very few go to full 'control'), the tacit assumption is that it would cut down bias, increase diversity, check the corporate interests of the owners and the managerial interests of the editors and, to boot, infuse values of creativity and spontaneity.

The mental mix in which such assumptions are embedded stems from beliefs in goodness as inversely correlated with status, part of that goodness being 'diversity'. The mix also has a strong anti-bureaucratic, anti-organisational element in it: managerial or organisational skills are not considered as 'proper ones'. (Compare the Liberal ideologue who sees, by definition, public sector/bureaucratic efforts as 'unproductive'.)

'Rights', to be sure, come into it but not very often as terminal. Rather they are thought of as instrumental. It is a fascinating and important conception. Crudely, the image is one of the owners selling out or the owners necessarily having to undermine the old bourgeois ideals of press freedom. The editors and working journalists, not so closely tied to property, come to the rescue to restore them.

After the 1975 journalists' protests and strikes on the *Australian*, in reaction to what many journalists took to be deliberate anti-Labor slanting and anti-Labor rewriting of stories, Rupert Murdoch commented that not only was it just a few malcontents, but that in any case all he was doing was cutting out *their* 'bias'.

It is a striking instance of how low serious consideration of media issues in Australia has sunk that no one took up this comment as a general issue. To rule it out of court in the given context is one thing; quite another to rule it out of court as such. The importance of Murdoch's point holds whatever his reasons for making it, whatever his self-interest and whatever be 'the truth' about 1975. An approach which does not even inquire into what ideological, distorting, self-interest and self-deceptive influences might exist amongst editors, managers, journalists, printers, the academics who study media and the reformers who want to change them, but asks such questions only about proprietors, is not the best for which we can strive. 'Independence' is 'bad' when top dogs try to exercise it. 'Dependence' is 'good' if presented in terms of control-from-below by journalists, and maybe printers, on proprietors. Its supposedly grassroots origins are sufficient to ennoble the content.

Whether, and in what ways, 'diversity' is related to various conceivable kinds of journalists' or journalists-and-printers' power or to other forms of institutionalised or de facto checks on proprietors (trusts, external boards, corporate practices, guarantees of editorial autonomy) is surely not such a simple issue.

Salvation from below?

The key theme of creativity and diversity, emerging from the bottom but stifled by homogenising owners and bureaucrats, occurs in many contexts. Snatches of it weave like a plaintive air in and out of discussion and casual comment. It would need a very careful ethnographic study to track down its many forms and assess their importance.

It occurs most commonly in newspapers and the ABC. However, for the SBS one hears of cold WASP bureaucrats vs warm, spontaneous and culturally authentic ethnic communities (except those whose cultural habits raise your blood pressure). In the satellite and networking controversies of the last few years, some of the more imaginative anti-Packerites and anti-capital city people have found charm, spontaneity and localism in regional TV interests, who yesterday would have represented only Marx's 'idiocy of rural life'.

The theme of journalists exercising de facto power and undermining the formal authority of owners, managers and editors from some kind of anti-authority, counter-hegemonic or 'adversary' position crop up only in loose and fragmentary bits. Yet they are frequent.

The 'extreme right' version is of interest only marginally for work on conspiracy theories, myths, and the techniques of 'angling'. The work on the complaints of business against the press needs comparative analysis. How far are the themes there similar to standard themes of anti-trade union bias? And why is the anti-business bias theme hardly existent here, mild in the UK, and fairly strong in the US? Are these themes related to the standard one about young, active, questioning, 'idealistic' journalists being 'naturally' on 'the left'? Are they related to work on the adversary culture, on the clash between presidency and press, or on the alleged undermining of rural values by capital city centred TV?

In Australia such themes find faint and distorted echoes in talk about the press gallery, about ABC journalists and in fairly regular titbits from B.A. Santamaria, who sees 'anarcho-Marxism' in sections of the media.

One can tease out the sort of questions which are discernible in this murky mess: What are the forms of resistance to proprietorial and editorial norms open to and practised by some journalists? What are the sociological and psychological correlates differentiating such journalists from those who obey? What trade-offs or compromises must both kinds make? If such forms of resistance can be found, what is their political content? In what sense are they 'adversary' to the existing culture? In what sense are they 'counter-hegemonic'? What sort of media and media practices weaken, undermine, challenge which structural aspects of the social system?

The main stress in recent years has been on debunking the

old watchdog critical journalism notion, on focusing on what are taken to be supportive, stabilising, legitimising, reproductive media aspects. The key themes suggested by the matters alluded to are de facto checks on one-way top-down communication processes, and whether and how they introduce manifest or latent forms of diversity into the final product. If one takes the notion of a counter-culture, an adversary culture, or anti-hegemony seriously, then work on what resists and counteracts, on the disruptive and discontinuous, takes on a new meaning. For the forms of resistance, if such they are, are not traditional forms of (class) struggle—we are not talking here of strikes.

One should look with a fresh and cultural eye at the ties of journalists with professionally destructive or pseudo destructive tendencies in the system, and a critical look at concepts of legitimation, delegitimation and reproduction: How do such notions relate to Schumpeter's 'creative destruction' ideas? This would involve serious work, of which there is very little, on the notion of hegemony and especially 'anti-hegemony'.

Public broadcasting

Media complexes, which are at least formally 'different', will have an unknown diversifying input into the total system. They may be internally heterogeneous. How important one believes they are depends very much on one's time scale and on one's general view of how power, influence, knowledge and values interrelate and what their importance is in relation to other available analytical categories, for example the labour process, class, ownership.

'Public broadcasters are clearly marginal' is incontestable only if you pre-suppose the commercial mass-market criteria, which put emphasis on numbers. The commercial game has two major aspects: numbers and time. It is an ahistorical before/after, on/off game. If you change the rules, then you can look at public broadcasters (or given programs) in relation to a narrowcasting concept. Once you go for market segmentation, which you can call 'community appeal', you have endless ploys which show that such and such a station is 'important' in relation to given groups or networks. The standard argument, never tested, is that PFPEFL (Program for Potato Eating Frog Lovers) not merely voices their views about the injustices and forms of exploitation they suffer from. Even if they were the only ones to ever tune in, it legitimises them at least in their own eyes. This helps to give them strength and self-confidence. This in turn, and so on.

The time aspect is even more easily brought into play: Station X broadcasts to a tertiary elite. When that gets jobs and power (still tacitly assumed) its youthful influences will manifest themselves. This is the 'leaders-of-tomorrow' move.

How much truth there is in any of this, and by what means one might check on the claims, can be left to others. Is it possible to take the 'spiral of silence' approach of Elisabeth Noelle-Neumann (1974) and reverse it for public broadcasters?

Charting media 'diversity'

There is not much dispute about the key assumption of the traditional line of argument, related to J.S. Mill, which tries to link diversity and democracy. It is in terms of the presentation and knowledge not of 'mere variety' but of 'diversities' which are related to citizen-relevant, important, worthwhile, significant alternatives, options and choices. Once that has taken place the next steps in the process—the battle, clash, conflict of options—and the outcome—rationally tested, cleansed-and-tried truth—move to the centre of the stage.

The better work on the left is related to this conception of significant alternatives. That work, at its most superficial, simply argues that position, interests, movements and struggles of one side (workers) are being heavily discriminated against in and by the media. It then gives an account of why this is so in terms of a bipolar class conflict conception.

This view fuses two contentions: You can agree, for instance, with much of what it says about the most frequently used case, that of strikes and the media treatment of industrial relations. You can then try to give an account of causes in terms of numerous variables, none of which is 'basic'. Amongst these there could be either class conflict as a 'factor' with differential case-to-case weight or the rejection of the notion of 'class' and the attempt to work out some other conflict model.

Whatever one's view about this fusion of what happens and why it happens, the best work on the left goes much beyond it. It sets out to show what the bourgeois concept of 'significant diversities' is concerned with. It would, taking the strike/union issue or issues such as sexism or racism, try to link their treatment in the media with conflicts of interest and, in turn, link these with struggles over hierarchy and with concepts of exploitation and domination. It would conclude by arguing that the media treatment of X is an instance of social system choices not being 'on the agenda', or alternative social systems being 'distorted' or caricatures. It will, thus, attempt to link 'sexism' or 'racism' with 'capitalism'. Its main concern is with systemic diversity. It wishes to focus on this and highlight the absence of a capitalism/socialism media option. It has rarely paid much attention to diversities marginal for it.

The study of media diversity, within-media and between-media, if it is related to democratic theory, must be the study of significant alternatives. Since there is no agreement on 'significant' or what is an 'alternative', one is stuck from the start.

The more radical (in the sense of claiming to go to the root of taken-for-granted conventions and of language which embodies them) a possible option or alternative is, the harder it will be to think of relevant diversities within the system(s) it claims to be opposed to. Consider this point in relation to Mary Daly's *Gyn/Ecology* which she sees as a book 'written in a situation of extremity, written on the edge of a culture that is killing itself and all of sentient life'.

Arguments about media legitimating a given social order are usually fused with the contention that, if they do so, they also assist in putting some other order out of court. 'If the media legitimate and help to reproduce capitalism, they exclude socialism from the choice of options.' This seems reasonable as a general argument so long as it is realised that the issue of what the content of 'the option' is is a separate one. X may be excluded, X is a formal option, but is X a 'genuine' option? If you believe (say) that the only possible choice is between 'private capitalism' and 'state capitalism' or 'bureaucratic collectivism', your view as to what the nature of the 'options' at stake might be is likely to be different from those who do not agree with this analysis. Consider the debate about the relationship of feminism or gay liberation to various social systems.

Issues about what are and are not real differences within one movement, and whether generic issues are meaningful, cannot be avoided. As we were thinking about this, a colleague commenting on Beatrice Faust's *Women, Sex and Pornography* said that the book set up a strawperson of 'women's liberationists' views and ignored or played down important differences in the movement on the issues discussed. We all make, inevitably, comments of this kind. Serious work often raises issues as to whether a generic approach to what is widely known as an entity with an essence or essences is justified (compare the debate over whether one can speak of a generic fascism in Larsen et al. (eds) 1980).

Television

The usual way to define diversity on TV (or radio) is in terms of the number of different kinds of programs available so that, if you have an extra hour of public affairs and an hour less of detective drama, diversity is said to have increased. It is easy to show that this breaks down at once (Owen 1978).

Even if you ignore the key criticism of content analysis—that it has a positivist view of 'meaning' being self-evident on the surface of the material, hence sees no need for a theory of signification—there is no way in which you can decide *apart* from theoretical decision what content is 'significant' and 'relevant' to social structure. If that major obstacle is ignored, there are still no criteria within a range of surface 'reasonable' choices by which you can work out how many and what program categories to use.

The best US study, by Dominick and Pearce (1976), shows a decline in 'diversity' by showing that a higher proportion of prime time programming is increasingly devoted to fewer, and especially to three key, categories. But the classification and coding rest on program descriptions, thus ignoring the visual dimension. If the categories, which in any case overlap, are redefined, the results must differ. Like the analysis of newspapers, such content analysis entirely begs the question of audience response.

There is a wide range of 'sensible' categories for content analysis (Sterling and Haight 1978; McQuail 1977) but no theory-based decision criteria. You can look at 'diversity' in terms derived from ratings, or needs and gratification approaches. However, the major standard references yield but little. Few studies take account of viewing and usage in context (but compare Lull 1980a, 1980b). But not all is gloom. With the growth of more specific audiences, and the future use of narrowcasting, we will get many more studies on the lines of Frank and Greenberg (1980), who link uses and gratification and market segmentation approaches and then relate TV usage to fourteen segments, the context in which it is viewed and how that is related to other communication behaviour. It is hardly accidental that the Corporation for Public Broadcasting assisted in funding the project.

What was up to now a 'minority' concern—how to assess the interests and intensities of non-commercial viewers and what kind of qualitative rating system might be appropriate for them—will flourish as a growing commercial field with the impossibility of using conventional methods for cable and pay TV and with multiple sets and audience fragmentation.

Ownership, oligopoly, diversity

Though cautiously, this writer used in his early work to subscribe to, and helped to spread, the traditional arguments linking growing concentration of ownership (oligopoly, dupoly, or monopoly) with diminishing diversity of media content. The arguments are widely accepted, and very 'respectable' in the sense that they are standard academic and royal commission/public inquiry fare. We have been unhappy about them for some years.

The standard arguments, which supposedly link concentration or spread of ownership with lesser and greater diversity, stress one or more of three roughly distinguishable strands: A power strand, an occupational choice/autonomy strand, and owner-content diversity strand. In most arguments these three tend to get mixed up. The power strand may or may not refer to diversity of content.

Power

This tends to run like this: Ownership and control of the media bring with them various and major forms of both power and influences. This is true of any given single medium and becomes even more important if we look at cross-ownership. Ownership concentration means power concentration.

There is no objection here to such views at the most general level. Disputes occur over the definition, degree and extent of power: what are the relations between potential power and its exercise; the question of how one may discover and assess invisible power; its relations to concepts of the ruling class or elite; the divisions or factions amongst the owners or rulers and their relations to media content.

If you hold a ruling class or elite view, it is not easy to see how you might be concerned with the numbers or composition of the class or elite as such unless related to other concerns—possibilities affecting content of media, or class struggle, or counter-hegemony.

The obsession with a few people is in terms of what they might do with their papers in an election. It is with the most bourgeois of all processes and institutions—elections, parliaments, parties—which in other contexts are often pictured as important fig leaves for class rule.

Why this obsession? Our guess—there is no possible evidence of even the faintest kind—is that it gives vent to frustrations and disgust which follow from the overall lack of popular interest in media and media reform and from the great difficulties of achieving even the most tokenistic and marginal of reforms.

A media proprietor cushioned by monopoly can act more arbitrarily and more powerfully. But such an attack on concentration is not linked with diversity in any way. There is a vast range of things most people would see as more diverse, which papers could run while making more money and increasing the owner's power.

To repeat: There is nothing in the extreme case—a single owner of all print media with cross interests in others—which enables you to predict how the interests to be advanced will be advanced. A single Fairfax does not equal a single Murdoch nor a single Herald and Weekly Times.

Hence the concentration of power argument is a straight out political point in terms of democratic theory; it is an objection to having a private and non-elected Ministry of Truth. It is essential to stress (as we have always done) that what is being attacked here is private concentration of power which can be used arbitrarily, and that the attack does not hinge on what is actually done or whether it increases or decreases diversity. If one person owned all papers and decided to support, in diverse ways, your top 'good' cause, you would still have to oppose their monopoly. The key point is that the argument from principle in terms of a procedural concept of democracy will leave most people cold and cuts no political ice.

Occupational Choice

This runs in terms of: Journalists should be as autonomous as possible, with the perfect paradigm being a free-floating socially uninfluenced person who consults nought but his or her conscience. This is the Polonius model from *Hamlet*: 'This above all: to thine own self be true'. More and separate owners, it is said, increase the chances of this happening, of countering pressures or orders seen as counter to the ethics of journalism. If there is concentration, then alternative employment opportunities are cut. More theoretically, independent entry points into and within the media system are positively related to reducing the costs of being autonomous.

By the nature of the case, relevant material on the point must be anecdotal. If it holds, then it also is the case that journalists have more 'play' and are much less socialised, constrained, cowed and manipulated than they are often said to be in other contexts.

The chief empirical point is how separate ownership relates to what separate employers are likely to wish for, and to informal but effective arrangements such as blacklists. Do institutions which are legally separate give greater chances to those who have rocked the boat should they wish to move? One thinks of the very effective grapevine against 'troublemakers' across formally separate institutions.

The occupational choice argument may have something to it. Once you consider the way journalists actually work and think of their work and the wide range of informal processes which work against 'troublemakers', it becomes difficult to make 'too much' of the argument. But, since it is not possible to study this systematically, there is no way we know which will help in finding out how much one should make of it. We have no way of comparing sanctions, let alone 'self-censorship', in separately owned media enterprises systematically with joint, cross, and common ownership patterns. It is hard to imagine how one could be systematic about editorial and proprietoral personalities and 'bring in' size of firm, circulation, degree of employment changes in other media or in public relations and so on.

Ownership pluralism and message pluralism

In the United States, there is a good deal of concentration-and-content work. When you examine coverage of stories, not surprisingly you tend to get higher commonalities than when you use more general and abstract measures. Thus, when a 'story' is more tightly defined, it turns out that close to 70 per cent of stories covered in the weekday evening newscasts by one network are covered by at least one of the other two (Lemert 1974). But if you stress content commonalities of the broad kind for 'stories', then 95 per cent of the time US television news editors select stories characterised by conflict, proximity, timeliness, and the availability of film (Buckalew 1969–70).

Studies of varying degrees of honesty and sophistication keep on trickling out in the US. By citing those you wish to cite, you can 'prove' the point you want to make. Gormley (1976) made a major, thorough, and sophisticated attempt to link cross-ownership with news homogeneity. Critics of cross-ownership have commonly cited his short *Columbia Journalism Review* version, but the book presents a much more complex picture. Nor can Gormley claim that all co-operation is 'bad'. His technically excellent study shows the limits of a positivist method. He can measure overlap and, up to a point, co-operation, but there is no way given his paradigm that he can distinguish between 'good' and 'bad' forms, nor decide the point at which it becomes a vice because it is carried 'too far'. Not surprisingly, the case studies cannot and do not permit any conclusions unless one includes as 'case study' anecdotal material which, by definition, does not touch on multiple variables or comparisons.

A 1974 Rand study meticulously summarised the evidence thus far, and concluded that there is no proof for most questions about the effects of media concentration on media performance (Baer et al.): 'The form of media ownership generally seems to have a small impact on economic or content performance . . . Differences reported in certain studies have not been reproduced in other situations.' For cross-ownership 'no significant differences' in economic or quantity of programming effects are seen. For the press, as far as the US studies go, the bulk of them have found few differences and no relation between ownership, lack of competition and 'inferior' journalism (Compaine 1979).

The US studies are inconclusive and have not shown any systematic relation between ownership pluralism and content pluralism. In the absence of a general theory, we must ask many crucial questions: What are the co-operative practices which exist and how far do they undermine or qualify formal independence and create interdependencies? What are the conflictual practices which interfere with smooth interaction within one firm or different types of media owned by that firm? What kinds of markets are these media in and how far, and in what sense, is there 'diversity' in them? If there is, who can alter it and introduce greater or lesser degrees of it?

And: What happens if we (temporarily) shift the focus from owners to journalists, editors and middle management? Such a shift means major attention to source-reporter relations, to resources which make the achievement of diversity more or less likely and, to be sure, to the effects on journalists of beliefs they have about owners and editors and type of story usage.

Conclusion

This paper is very depressing. Our only plea is that it was even more depressing to think through and to write than it will be to read. It asserts that:

(a) No reliable guardians of media diversity can be located. If your main objective is its achievement you will have to work with all kinds of people and interests you might find ideologically and personally repugnant and oppose many whom you on other grounds approve of. In clashes within the media, private or national, and between types of media, and between media and governments, those who wish to optimise diversity have no permanent enemies or allies. The contrast between 'principle' and 'pragmatism' or 'expediency' is invalid in this field. There are no guardians of diversity nor best bets over time. Those on the side of diversity need not so much a lot of long spoons so as to sup with devils; rather, their problem is that all their allies are Janus-faced. Angels become devils overnight and vice versa.

(b) We, and most of the people we talk to, are pretty certain that we know media diversity when we see it, read it, or listen to it. Yet, as soon as one even glances at the concept of diversity as such, endless problems seem to arise.

(c) We, and most of the people we talk to, are also pretty certain that some Australian media firms are more interventionist and more likely to impose uniformity than others. Of the three present major oligopolists most agree Murdoch is the most interventionist, but his founding of the *Australian* means that at one time he was the primary ally for increasing diversity. Australian critics, since they hate Murdoch so much for being what he is and for 1975, never allude to the fact that many people in New York think he has improved *Village Voice* with more and better staff and resources and little of the intervention he stands so widely condemned for.

(d) The standard ways of looking at oligopoly and diversity seem weak since they overstress purely formal or legal arrangements and neglect informal arrangements. We repeat that this works both ways: The formal interdependency might be counteracted by informal conflict and vice versa. They are also weak since they pay little attention to the processing of the raw material transformed into news by journalists.

Why some existing firms have different practices re whatever diversity they go in for must also be studied in a way which looks at their context and its constraints and, so far as one may, at personal factors applying to decision makers.

There is nothing in the paper to suggest that a general theory of the relation between ownership pluralism and message pluralism is at all likely. And, to be sure, in any given case the critics may be right. The range of conditions under which fewer owners mean less diversity may indeed exist—nothing written here runs counter to that.

This paper will fall flat. People who are interested in the issues it raises are mostly politically concerned or engaged. The diversity of content argument is one of the very few things critics of the media have going for them. If they argue in those terms, they have some chance of making the matter justifiable, and acquiring 'standing'. Thus, even if all we said was infallible and 101 per cent sure—and it is neither—it would be rejected.

Is everything as before? We leave that to you.

Dilemmas of Freedom and Policy

4 Dilemmas of Mass Media Policies

The Canberra-based Academy of the Social Sciences asked Henry to give its annual lecture in 1979. Here Henry was principally addressing eminent social science intellectuals, who were not well versed in media studies, and so dealt with what Henry considered were intellectuals' misconceptions about media and their audiences. It also raised issues of the broadest significance, especially how media related to citizenship, how information flow was crucial to informed choice, but also how participation in media issues, especially before the recent Broadcasting Tribunal inquiries, had given many their first experience of citizenship. It speculates on future trends in the press, notably the polarisation between quality and entertainment papers, and the growing importance of a new equity issue—the gap between the information rich and information poor. It concludes with a consideration of the rationales underlying official intervention in this field, and how they rest either on shoddy foundations or are becoming increasingly problematic.

This chapter examines the broad 'rationales' underlying government activity and policies in the mass media and communications fields. There are three main points. First, the existing arguments for regulating the broadcast media are rapidly being undermined. New grounds for regulation—or deregulation—will have to be worked out. Second, the arguments against government intervention in the press are being eroded as the distinction between printed matter and broadcasting becomes blurred. A section of the press—I stress 'a section'—shows a few of the characteristics associated with arguments for 'freedom of the press'. We are moving towards a split between 'quality' and 'entertainment' press. The entertainment press will drag down the freedom of the quality press and newspapers will be more controlled as a whole if any of them are so. Third, there are complex links between freedom of the quality press, broadcasting policy and the concept of citizenship. But in future we face a growing division between well-informed, skilled, more rational citizens relying on excellent papers and poorly informed heavy TV watchers devoted to entertainment papers with a minimal chance of developing their reason.

The Elusive Impact of Broadcasting

The media issues on the political agenda do not form a clear pattern. They are incoherent, muddled. Many become visible for only a short while. It is hard to judge how widespread are the roots of a given issue, let alone how deep they go. Media specialists who are mostly tertiary trained and tend to be professional wordsmiths, who make careers by justifying distinctions, tend to exaggerate vastly how widely one of their own favourite concerns about media is shared.

For some years the ABC's *Broadband/Lateline* was the most controversial of its programs if one judged by what one's academic colleagues argued about. One got the impression that one could and should judge the giant ABC by one tiny section on radio—*Broadband* or *Lateline*. One was labelled 'right' or 'left' depending on one's attitude towards this program. Supporters of the program saw every new cut as evidence that it was hurting the ruling class and 'the system'. Opponents tended to be even more absurd: they often saw the program as a menacing cancer, bound to spread if not rooted out, wasting public money so as to push an 'extreme left' line which was a real threat to 'the system'. Its continued toleration was symbolic of the ABC management's lack of backbone if not of the decay of the soft society. While all this huffing and puffing went on, a 1978 ABC survey showed that 84.8 per cent of respondents had never heard of the program. Of the 15.2 per cent who had, only 53.4 per cent had listened to it at some time. When there was 'a threat' to the ABC's symphony orchestras some years ago, one would have thought that a national crisis had occurred.

A 1979 ABC Sydney–Melbourne survey found 67 per cent of respondents did not associate the ABC with these concerts.

Though there is little hard evidence on the point, it seems that media specialists and those interested in the media badly underestimate the purely passive reactions of many people to most of the media. While the average time spent viewing commercial TV during a week is 18 hours and 27 minutes per person in the six capital cities, there is a striking negative correlation between the amount of TV viewing and the level of occupation and income.

Thus the intelligentsia have scarcely realised that the average time spent on commercial TV is around nine years of a life, of which about two years are spent attending to the advertisements. If and when they discover such facts and come to believe them, they tend to brand them with superficial labels like 'brainwashing' or 'manipulation' or 'media hegemony'. These are little more than a revival of the discredited needle-injection view of the power of the media, with hegemony apparently a superior kind of slow-drip injector. Lenin thought the proletarian vanguard might inject revolutionary consciousness into the working class. Here the oligopolist class fraction is seen as injecting the viewers with 'false consciousness', harmful effects or passivity. Nothing makes Australian academics more angry than the standard comment by the commercial network spokesmen that people can surely switch off. The 'can' begs, surely, a host of questions. Yet the anger aroused by it, or even more by the phrase 'we only give them what they want', is highly significant.

Unfortunately, the heat is not offset by much helpful light from the surveys of media preferences and consumers' complaints. They are too often marred by questions presenting false alternatives in hypothetical contexts constructed upon unreal or unstated assumptions.

Still, you can get a relatively clear picture now and then. Surveys, evidence to tribunals, the attitudes of the more forward-looking people in the TV industry and the reaction of active reformers all indicate that there is now genuine and widespread concern about children's TV. The small proportion of active people in this field give expression to a much more widely felt unease apparently lasting but not very intense—usually not intense enough to produce many calls or letters, let alone submissions. The commercial lobby, FACTS, has no difficulty in showing that the overt complaints, as measured by protests to the stations or submissions to the Tribunal, amount to something between 1000 and 3000 a year, compared to its stations' penetration of nearly four million homes a week. The complainants are a tiny proportion of all viewers. When it is in one of its less intelligent moods—this gambit is now going out of fashion—the group can, correctly, talk about minorities and argue, questionably, that they are not 'representative' and that hence there is no 'problem'. If this means that the uneasy viewers who worry about children's TV do not back the active minority in words, in surveys, it is false. As in so many other fields, most people have no worked-out policy, they have feelings that 'something ought to be done'. They leave the details to the reformers and to the Tribunal.

It is true that the activists do not have a mandate in any formal sense. There are no elective processes in such situations. Whether they are seen as 'representative' of a large proportion who broadly sympathise with their endeavours or, at least verbally, endorse them if asked, depends on what theory of 'representation' one holds. The links between the minority of activists, a given institution (the Australian Broadcasting Tribunal) and the 'public'—here the viewers and parents—will always be uncertain. But, to the extent that survey evidence truly reflects opinions, the activists' views are certainly representative.

In general, however, consumer reaction to the media is, by the very nature of the relationship, extremely hard to assess. What little information we have about the quantity of overt complaint may be misleading. The annual published figures for written complaints to the Tribunal are low. Reformers generally argue that if it were easier to complain the number of complaints would rise: they put the blame on the stations. It is probably true that if stations promoted complaints procedures with the glamour and skill of commercial advertising—for example with an identifiable Ms Fixit giving feedback on the results—there would be more complaints. But not many more, and these disproportionately of the kind that intellectuals dismiss as trivial though stations consider them important:

objections to clothes, language, plots, viewing times, program clashes, and the like.

The quality of complaints to date makes assessment even more difficult. Every day, for example, many complaints about TV reach the wrong channel. The ABC gets complaints about commercial TV shows and Channel 7 about shows on Channels 9 and 10. Viewers become very angry when this is pointed out. Perhaps the most surprising kind of complaint is that the viewer's favourite program has been shifted—when it has not. A dispassionate and sensitive study of the record of complaints—neither patronising nor whitewashing the viewers—would be a worthwhile enterprise; but the results would probably be very depressing for any believer in the spread of rationality and intelligence in society.

Press freedom, informed choice and citizenship

The venerable issues about the press—choice, bias, diversity, oligopoly, ties with other media, cross-ownership, relation to the social system and its legitimation and reproduction—are hard even to list without a yawn. Except for some recent very able Marxist contributions on the last point, which are mistakenly cast as answers instead of questions, little fresh about them has been said for decades.

Yet insofar as any of these issues is publicly discussed in Australia and the discussion is reported in the press, it now takes place in a context dominated by a statutory body linked with government. Moreover, this is a body concerned with broadcasting. It is significant of the changing context of discussion that what were once press issues in relation to TV should now have to be raised as a TV issue in relation to the press. Discussion is increasingly dominated by TV partly because of its inherent strengths and partly because the question of the government's role invariably arises in relation to TV.

Accuracy and reliability of news and information are at the core of the self-image of the press. At least that holds for those papers which set out to offer more than entertainment. These claims are at the centre of the argument against governments intervening in the press. That argument in turn is tied loosely to vague notions about the place of the press in a democratic society.

The rationale centres upon the information role of the press and covers various kinds of information. Some might help you to cope better (= 'more reasonably') with your shipping schedule or your taxation form. Others may help you to understand better (= with more insight, refinement, knowledge, appreciation of skills—all of which are in loose ways tied to 'reason'). But the crucial claim is that the press provides digestible information which is relevant to one's citizenship. The main trouble with this formulation is that it calls for a disquisition on 'citizenship'. On a pronounced participatory view of democracy the citizen will be very different from the citizen envisaged in an indirect democracy run by elected, competing elites. The odds are that the champions of participation would not wish to grant the citizen label to the second type of person. At least they might wish to claim that such a 'citizen' is but a pale shadow of the genuine article. There are difficult, unresolved questions here about the amount and kind of information the citizen needs. The claim that some concept of information which enables people to become more knowledgeable, so assists in making them therefore more reasonable and thus make more choices, better informed, is at the core of the justification for freedom of the press. Even formulated in this loose way it is clear that the ideal implicit in this is connected with that of searching, inquiring, choosing, opting in some active way.

The assumption smuggled in is crucial: the better informed you are, the more reasonable you become, the more varied and many-splendoured your options and your choices. Room can be made for the fact that you may know more, be better informed and then restrict your choices, choose not to choose all these options and remain in the state in which you were before you acquired all this information and knowledge. This can be done by distinguishing between an uninformed, habitual traditionalism or conservatism and one adopted after you have looked calmly, rationally and full of information at the tempting options. 'Conservatives are stupid, unthinking creatures of habit. People who choose conservatism might be all right.' Habit equals unreason. Choice and implied discontinuity equal reason.

One must confess that it is not easy to find people who actually argue, think and (important here) feel that way: for a progressive the idea that someone might have looked honestly and critically at his sweet fruit and then rejected it is offensive. Conservatives are on the whole (certainly in Australia) very suspicious of people who look seriously at the options ('flirtation' may be all right) and then join their side. They do not trust them.

Knowledge based on information supplied by a serious press, linked with reason and choice, is of the essence. The level of knowledge, the type of knowledge and its assumed direction remain open. For some, for instance, knowledge 'points' to the support of capitalism, for others to its overthrow. If you decide to support the capitalist system those who see this as an outrageous decision will tend to find reasons why your support cannot be 'truly' reasonable. They may point to processes and structures in the system which distort your potential reason. In this context the press and TV figure as the main distorters and blockers of the very reason they claim to encourage—they are seen as at the core of the unreasonable system itself and as legitimising and reproducing it. Similarly those who claim to have endorsed socialism with open eyes can be labelled by supporters of capitalism as suffering from invincible ignorance so that they 'just don't understand' how economics, human nature, original sin, evil or the lessons of history work.

Neither side will allow the conditions of 'reasonable choice' it applies to itself to apply to the other. The choice made by the antagonist must be one which is the result of factors other than deliberation, accurate information and calm examination of options.

The press, then, provides the information you can process into choices which are more reasonable than they would be without it. The range of choices or what are seen as 'real' choices varies. There are people who think Lib vs Lab is a 'choice'. Others do not. Neither view is silly. There are also people who see 'no choice' between Bjelke Petersen's police and the KGB or Gestapo. They are stupid.

Given the assumed links of information–knowledge–

reason–action, if you are in a strongly felt distinctive and well-worked out minority position you will think, quite correctly, that our mainstream mass media do not present a wide range of alternatives and exclude many possible lifestyles. You will discover that the press takes the world as it is and makes it even more so. The Australian press rarely or never presents any form of laborism let alone socialism, no form of fascism, no form of cosmic consciousness or alternative technology or monastic Christianity or homosexuality or feminism as a possible and possibly reasonable option. The range of possible alternatives presented here is much narrower than are presented by mass media in other capitalist societies (Italy, France, Scandinavia or Israel).

The press has many other roles which one finds less frequently in rationales for its freedom: watchdog, crusader, moneymaker (one can see this as equivalent to freedom fighter), or provider of surveillance. All are tied to the information function.

Entertainment is not so tied; and a press that mainly entertains is frowned on. (Not so TV, nor magazines.) It is allowed to amuse, please and entertain but not 'merely' or 'mainly' so, without losing its special cachet: that's froth and bubble, lightweight flim flam. Governments may or may not leave it alone but it has no longer any special weight in or claims on our society. If a press with such a function is suppressed it would be, on this view, like stopping a juggler or composer of jingles.

Entertainment and wit and joy and amusement are not linked with press functions or freedom because they are not seen as linked with reason. A serious and informative press probes. It goes in for investigative journalism. A frothy light-hearted press digs for dirt for the sake of circulation and titillation. The *Age* exposes. That is linked to reason. *Truth* scandalises. It 'reveals' and that is linked to the low, the mean and the exploitative.

It should now be clear why people are so outraged when they see their cherished alternative not even mentioned by the mainstream media, or treated with contempt, or not taken seriously, or 'distorted'. There are many forms of anger with the press for ignoring, distorting or downgrading people's own version of reason and of what is to be done. The crudest kind is the notion that if the press were fairer and printed a lot about one's alternative a good many people would support it. Is it not reasonable and worthy of support? A truly Christian press would 'produce' Christians; a pro-Labor press would, telling the truth about Labor, increase the pro-Labor vote. A fair go for homosexuals would not only show that the 'problem' is one of hatred of them by 'straights' (homophobia) but would also increase the number of people who would adopt homosexuality themselves.

It is not, of course, simply a matter of 'capitalism'. Other capitalist societies show much greater variety within the main media, including the easily available daily papers. Here it is still the rule that the poor, the unemployed (this is changing very fast), the doctors, the lawyers, the politicians and the students get 'the treatment'. The Aboriginal image, the homosexual image, and to a much lesser extent the feminist image are now much more diversified in at least some papers than they were a few years ago. Professors, by the way, get remarkably good treatment in the main media, unless they are associated with technology, medicine or nuclear energy (for or against). Someone should really glance at why professors are so favoured: is it because they can combine being dull and safe with being exotic, being freakish, having verbal authority but no power or serious influence, and possessing high status?

Unless at least the serious papers more regularly give space to unconventional options, more and more sections will come to believe that the press not only does not, but cannot, 'represent' them. They have versions of the truth as they see it. They expect that the information–knowledge–reason–action promise will work for them. In a society in which there are so many conflicting versions of what the content of reasonable action should be, the promise implied by the freedom of the press rationale is ever more difficult to fulfil. Many of the demands could only be met if the papers were much more expensive, had much more versatile staffs, were much more self-critical, had ways of selecting the potentially interesting from the merely fashionable and had much more space and time.

Not all can be accommodated in a daily as it now stands. If newspapers do not tackle these as major problems and explain what they can and cannot do, what it costs to do it, what the alternatives are if they cannot satisfy a demand, their support will shrink even further. They deceive themselves if they believe sales or lack of open opposition indicates 'support'. Their basis is much more fragile than they prefer to believe.

Bipolarity and policy

People who are interested in newspapers have little trouble in making judgments about them. Their verdicts are bipolar: top/bottom; pretty good/unspeakable; a real paper/a rag. These crude judgments are usually based on limited comparisons: people do not feel a need to read all capital city papers (regionals are never even considered) and to arrive at some rank order with the middling papers nicely placed. The appraisals of all but the few top papers tend to be unfair to those outside one's own state. They do not cope well with problems of commensurability between a state-based and a national press. (How many appraisals about 'Australia' let alone 'the world' would one make were one to take commensurability seriously?)

The appraisals are partly a function of familiarity: when last in London I read the *Sun* and the incredible *Star* for a while, and returned with a very different impression of where rock bottom lay: my Australian candidate(s) for it suddenly seemed (for a while) not so bad after all. The appraisals also ignore resources, population, circulation.

We can gauge newspapers by one main function—that which justifies the 'freedom of the press'—the provision of information enabling citizens to be better and more reasonably informed in making political and social judgments which are assumed to have links with action and with options. On this basis, one can grade the papers as top, middling, bottom. However, the coming decades are only too likely to see a squeezing out of the 'middling' papers. We may end up with a starkly bipolar structure: a very few political papers read mostly by well-educated and already well-informed citizens; and many papers with almost no political content as now defined—let's call them the entertainment papers. The latter papers may well survive on entertainment and the provision of information in non-political fields.

Tomorrow's quality papers will be very much better than today's, more 'balanced', more expensive and much more specialised. They will hardly be read by any but a fairly select elite, though available to all. They will provide all kinds of information and services from home and from abroad, via databanks and satellites eventually linked with pay TV and (de)scramblers. They will invite reader participation. The socialist ideal stemming from Bert Brecht—that communication in the best sense must not be of the sender/receiver, active/passive kind, but be reciprocal and complementary—will be realised in a very different way and with quite different results from those he expected. It will increase inequality.

The elite political papers will be more specialised, and will appeal to groups of readers with higher education, a need to know and a need for reliable and fast information. For them the effort needed to become a well-informed citizen will pay off. Economies of scale and the abolition of costs for distances (satellite) will mean that the best papers will have access to material of higher quality than is available to most existing continuing education bodies.

Few academics have explored the potential of the best journalism. Most tend to look down on it and have little idea of how it works or how to judge it. The future quality daily will use some academics. Because of limitations on space and time and the demands on its readers' time, it cannot become a daily *New Scientist*. But it can do some of the things such excellent magazines achieve week by week, and some new things. Supplements, special features, links via home communication centres with video-conferences and TV—all can and will be explored.

'The press' as a whole is constantly criticised. Here it is charged that it has failed to meet most of the functions the early democrats imputed to it. Owners and editors usually defend 'the press' as a whole: the same proprietors may own a rag and a good paper. Dog does not eat dog. Yet while the reasonable papers maintain solidarity with the rest they will not be able to build a strong constituency of their own which gives them critical, intelligent and conditional support.

In the years ahead it will be even easier to get hold of many versions of reality, to examine many agendas and to scan for basic criticisms of the social system. But whosoever hath, to him (and her) shall be given: It is the more educated and more skilled and more powerful who will be overwhelmingly the beneficiaries of these changes. It is they who will mostly use the elite papers. Diversity, plurality, accuracy, truth, investigation will be theirs. These boons will be formally available to all—the coming leaders among the powerless will be aware of this. Though it will be easy to buy and use these excellent papers, the burden of coping with their riches will be too great for many. The less educated, less skilled and less powerful, many of them long unemployed, will escape to the entertainment sheets and into popular TV and radio.

Print information however skilfully presented takes more time and interest to absorb than information conveyed by TV, which may not be 'absorbed' at all. Print is linked, at least in its more specialised content, with search and information processing habits which presuppose a strong desire for or interest in the material. You can go over printed material again and again and control the pace. For the readers of what are now the middling papers TV is ideal as the burden of processing political news increases: shorter items, more fragmentation, a visual presence. This is a major apparent substitute for checking. It gives the illusion of accuracy and truth through its mode of presentation: 'I saw it with my own eyes'. Such readers are likely to be disproportionately in the income and education groups who are already medium-heavy TV watchers.

The hope underpinning faith in democracy was that in time, with increasing information and education, the level of comprehension, involvement, and the quality of appraisal of the world would rise: education and information were the keys to the citizen's intelligence. This perspective overlooks the possibility that what has to be understood may get more and more difficult. The complexities of politics and the level of understanding needed to cope with them rise year by year. The burden becomes heavier. If you stand still you fall further and further behind.

The middling papers, should they try to move upmarket, will not be able to compete with the power of television and the fact that first thing in the morning you can get a brief and painless version of 'the news' from radio. As the middling papers will be forced downmarket and towards carrying less and less political information they may cut out politics. More likely they will disguise this by treating it purely in personality terms. Politicians will appear only as villains, victims of assassinations, actors in stories about sex.

For our theme it is unimportant whether politics in terms of issues, problems and alternatives is cut out or appears only in the guise of star and drama material. It is undeniable that you cannot judge the merits of a policy in terms of personalities as presented by the media. One might contend that politics is partly a question of trust and confidence in leaders, hence it is legitimate for the media to concentrate on them as people. But the media present an entirely managed, fabricated 'image' of politicians. The more popular the medium, the fewer warnings there will be that the whole enterprise is staged. It is quite impossible to draw even minimal inferences about policy from press or TV appearances. Nor can they provide the slightest trustworthy grounds for deciding whether a political figure deserves 'trust'.

Some print media can be used to show at length the complex possible relations of personality to policy: books can explore these relationships, but they cannot be judged through TV images or by reflecting on tiny news items, or photographs in the papers.

Government intervention in 'the press' does not follow from the press's partial failure to live up to the rationale for non-intervention. That merely offers an excuse; but it is very likely that future governments will wish to intervene. One reason is that the legal, constitutional, economic and conceptual boundaries between print and broadcasting are weakening. Teletext and interactive Viewdata signal an era in which electronic newspapers and the TV set as a major home communication centre will be normal. Print will operate in an electronic/broadcasting context which takes government intervention for granted.

If the new media are defined as 'broadcasting', the presumption is, by analogy, that government control is justified. If they are classed as 'narrowcasting', they can claim to be a 'press' where the opposite presumption applies. For us the main concern is with the political context. The right of governments to control broadcasting is not seen as anti-democratic. In most of

Europe the state plays a role in broadcasting which it does not have in the print media. When the ALP explored the feasibility of a paper run by a body similar to the ABC it was trying to argue from a medium in which government intervention is accepted to one where it is not. In the US attempts by broadcasters to shelter under the First Amendment have had little success.

Here state intervention in broadcasting is considerable. Statutory minimum times for religious broadcasting—one hour a week on radio, 1 per cent of time on TV—have existed for years. This embodies a right of access principle—applied only to religion. The Special Broadcasting Service, as the ALP and FACTS point out, is subject to a degree of direct government control unprecedented in our broadcasting system. It is the creation of a Liberal government. Classification, time zones and the amount of advertising are regulated. When FACTS complains about the 'C' programs for children, meaning regulation of content, and asks 'where will it stop?', it knows the answer: where FACTS can make it stop. There cannot be an a priori limit on the conditions to be attached to a TV licence. The stations of course want no conditions except technical ones, the 'traffic cop' idea, and those which keep newcomers and challengers out. Other people produce lists of all kinds of conditions they would like to see attached to licences. There is only one critical test for what constitutes the maximum viable conditions, even though it is beyond the bounds of political possibility: increase the range and weight of the conditions, suspend the need for ABT [Australian Broadcasting Tribunal] approval and allow a free market in licences. Let the market decide whether stations with such terrible conditions are worth buying and at what price.

The shift by the press into TV ownership and the shift to electronic newspapers will very much strengthen the general presumption that a right to regulate exists. The rationales of media control will shift in principle to favour regulation.

Should a future government decide to intervene, the defence of the press as a whole against control, in the name of 'freedom of the press', will carry no weight: the good papers to which the old rationale applied will be dragged down by the bad ones they did not criticise for decades. In protecting them now and associating with them as one entity, the quality papers are helping to dig their own grave.

The very important issues which today are largely academic—media oligopoly, cross-ownership and lack of overall political balance—will be a rope around the neck of the press once it is challenged on other grounds. It will not find many defenders: most people will not perceive a threat to it as a threat to their interests or freedom.

To avoid misunderstanding: the argument claims that the press as a whole has feet of clay should a government in the coming decades attempt to control it. It does not claim that this is bound to happen.

Can the better papers do much to avert this danger? They cannot be expected to make a formal denunciation of the others. Many come from their own stable. They would need to establish not just a distinct identity but reader loyalties of a kind no dailies here have ever sought. It would mean a very different attitude towards readers and a structure in which readers' rights and those of the paper are much more closely linked. They could give their readers many more chances to develop their potential citizenship and derive pleasure from it. They could constantly show that the interests of readers and their paper are partly linked. Defamation, freedom of information, accountability, defence of readers' rights—all these most bourgeois of causes could be championed in a coalition of quality papers and readers. It is not likely that even the best papers will attempt such changes.

These suggestions do not begin to touch on the problem of how to expand the constituency of good papers, how to induce more people to buy them. They amount only to a plea for the best sheep to separate themselves in their own interests from the goats, to nurture and interact with their shepherds and stop pretending that goats are sheep.

Broadcasting policy

Australian media-communications policy, if 'policy' means new legislation, is at present confined to broadcasting and the satellite. Some aspects of broadcasting policy have 'taken off' in the sense of involving a new range of people who have no evident self-interest at stake, have worked at their concern and attempted to inject it into policy, and have gone to a great deal of expense and trouble to make an impact.

The Gyngell-Strickland dispute,[1] for example, made 'accountability' and 'the rights of the public' into issues which went far beyond the manipulation and analysis of abstract concepts. The hearings and their reports became an experience which linked up with people's concepts of what they were and what they were specifically entitled to, what kind of say they ought to have. By the time Adelaide and Sydney hearings were over even the lawyers, in private, could see that there was something at stake for the 'public' which was not analysable in terms of, and hence not commensurable with, concepts of licensing and property rights. They found it hard to grasp what this something might be and hence tended to be even more dismissive of the concerns than they might otherwise have been.

Most of the public who appeared could not see that the stations had anything at stake, and refused to believe those who said that stations believed their licences were at some risk. Hence they were even more angry with the station representatives than they otherwise would have been: why were they so arrogant, petty, and contemptuous? Did they not see that there was 'no real threat'? Why would they not listen?

The reformers very rarely considered that stations and their owners and managers also might have concepts of 'selfhood' cast within a corporate context. It was inconceivable to them that station executives might feel genuine pride, concern and identification with the station, despair and anger at the ignorance of the industry on the part of the witnesses. They seemed like bloodlusting mosquitoes whose bites just might harm. Why should one lower one's dignity, waste time and incur high costs having to front up to such people?

The stations and their lawyers were ignorant of nearly all the work, reading and discussion, of the whole 'world' represented by the bulk of the public witnesses. They had no trouble in spotting sloppiness in their material. They focused on this. Having little direct acquaintance with the industry, the reformers seized on terms like 'fat profits' or 'greed' as substitutes for a rational critique. They had no reason to make allowances for all the real difficulties the industry faced—these were for most of them irrelevant. The ignorance by each side of the other was startling. When it emerged, each side blamed the other for not seeing what was self-evident, and for neglecting its 'duty to be informed'.

The hearings linked to broadcasting policy became in a convoluted, messy and imperfect way a process which fed back into the lives of many witnesses: these became, many of them for the first time, citizens—intermittent and partial, but citizens all the same. They made connections between what went on, what they thought should go on, what the slogans might mean and how they might gear their personalities to a participative practice.

It is hard to say what happened to the stations. They had all kinds of legal cocoons around them to insulate them from this strange and highly flawed learning experience. In any case they were, and had to be, very cautious in what they said. However, some of their more sensitive lawyers and managers learned that it might be good business and cost cutting not to try to make every post a winning post, to treat some of the critics more seriously, to find ways of listening which were not cast in such an aggressive mode.

Here we do not adopt the standpoint either of the standard reformer or of the industry, but let us examine the analysis put forward by the reformers.

The reformers' case puts major stress on the early promises of legislation to increase accountability and public participation; it stresses speeches by the chairman of the ABT and the minister, and what was expected from the 'promise of performance'. It then proceeds to ask: 'What went wrong?' and answers by allocating 'blame' or 'responsibility for failure' (the 'model' is cast in terms of an early norm and a later deviation from it, as the rot sets in). The government, the minister, Bruce Gyngell, the industry, particular people in it and, much more rarely, the Attorney-General's Department and, very rarely, the parliamentary draftsman, are found 'blameworthy'.

(The industry of course has an even cruder 'model', which starts with the early days as (unrealistic) deviance and the rest as a slow, painful, costly return to partial sanity, as the lawyers are 'unleashed' on the reformers who should never have been in the act in the first place. It has its own set of villains.)

The reformers' analysis then proceeds to stress very heavily the disillusionment, bitterness and withdrawal of many members of the public. We do not accept this framework as very enlightening. It leaves, by definition, the reasonableness of expectations out of account. It makes no attempt to investigate whether 'the public' should be seen as having not only rights, but also duties and responsibilities and, if so, how it measured up to them. It underrates the development of learning and citizen capacities and the emergence of a handful of people who became more capable as they went along. It tends to caricature the industry—to be sure, nowhere nearly as absurdly as the industry caricatures 'the public' at hearings.

The analytical map is, for our taste, not sufficiently self-critical and pays no serious attention to what was at stake and perceived to be at stake for the various parties. It is also not sufficiently sensitive to the problems of administration in a changing context. But most fundamentally, broadcasting, in some of its policy aspects, is linked in complex ways with how ordinary people experience some of the permanent concepts of political theory.

Crumbling rationales?

All the activity associated with the Tribunal processes presupposed the right of the government to enter the field and to regulate it. However, the rationales supporting this right may not be as strong as is widely taken for granted. With changes in technology, new interest in this field and a growing antipathy to regulation, it is likely that these rationales will further erode. There are five main rationales for regulation, which will be considered in turn.

1. Impact

This is the rationale on which governments have mostly relied, positing some power, disturbance, disequilibrium or other effect supposedly linked with broadcasting. It is claimed that in order to minimise or stop the 'harmful' impact, government must be able to control its source. The official case never provides any convincing evidence for the alleged impact, even though such evidence may exist. There are merely allegations open to endless challenges. For example, the rationale for restrictions in ethnic radio comprises 'common sense' statements about supposedly 'divisive' impacts. There is no evidence of the production of actual 'divisions' or indeed of whether 'divisiveness' is 'harmful', and if so to what or to whom.

On the other hand, in some cases where there is remarkably clear-cut evidence from social science it has little or no policy effect as such. There is a greater consensus on the harmful effects of TV violence on children than on many other social processes. Researchers, who have put years of effort into this field, who have seen their major findings repeatedly confirmed, and who care for children, tend to ascribe the lack of action to the power of the profitable TV industry and of the advertisers, or just to 'capitalism'. This is surely a major factor. The industry of course is quick to point out that consensus is not perfect. It knows also that social scientists tend to make findings with contextual qualifications, that children watch a good deal outside the 'children's TV' slots and that, in any case, it does not follow that if there is harm the government should prevent it—what of the parents?

The factor bolstering inaction which does not receive sufficient attention is that governments, let alone the general public, do not understand what social scientists can and cannot do. Just as 'I smoke three packets a day and look how healthy I am' is seen as a refutation of the cigarette–lung cancer linkage, so 'I watched TV a lot when young, lots of cartoons and films with violence. Look at me now—I seem OK' is taken to 'refute' all that 'academic nonsense'. Social scientists themselves cannot give an answer when asked about trade-offs. They cannot say how 'heavy' the effects will be in ten or twenty years. However good their work is—and in this field it is on the whole very good—it does not convince those who make policy decisions nor the public. It has little political weight.

If there were political rewards for 'discovering' this research then action, partly symbolic and partly tangible, would follow. But the uneasiness is not sufficiently focused or mobilised to have the force its proponents hope for. 'Impact' or 'effect' can be discovered or ignored at will with or without research. Recall President Nixon and the Commission on Obscenity, or Mr Fraser and the Human Relations Commission. The influence of social science research depends on whether it can be made to fit into a context of politics. It may in time help to establish such a context. Note—it has to be made to fit as a political act. But the notion that policy does or could 'derive' from research because of its scientific value is not worth discussing seriously.

2. Diversity

Small 'l' liberalism has the idea of mutually antagonistic diversity as its core: out of the clash, the competition of ideas, interests, values and lifestyles, something which has been tested and exposed to criticism, will emerge. It will be more rational since it will, after the test of exposure to conflicting views, be more 'truthful'.

It is easy to show that diversity cannot be a rationale for policy as soon as you glance at the concept. The point will be clear to all parents whose children can distinguish between pop groups and disco singers who 'all sound the same' to the parents. One assumes that a strongly assimilationist Australian hears the 30 to 45 language groups on ethnic radio as just indistinguishable gibberish. Research on comparative international TV programming has been blocked for decades by the varieties of classification.

Diversity is more manageable when equated with a unidimensional dichotomy. If you believe the crucial division in the media is between Liberal and Labor and also assume that there is a one-to-one relation between ownership and policy, the addition of a Labor-owned daily newspaper or TV station will increase diversity for you. Not so if you think 'both parties are interchangeable supporters of the system', nor if you start considering what Labor-owned radio has (not) done.

What Tony Staley has done, with enthusiasm and reasonable speed, is to pick out two demands—namely for 'public' and 'ethnic' broadcasting—which had been mobilised and which were not a threat to commercial stations, and make them into a policy of 'diversity'. (FARB, the Federation of Australian Radio Broadcasters, protested about audience fragmentation and 'double standards'—cries they now do not care to recall.) Since the system had been virtually frozen for decades, Staley's changes were relatively bold and innovative. The government hoped that public broadcasters would be 'different' in their programs—the law insists only that as an entity they do not live on advertising and are complementary to commercial stations. All the other aspects—community ties, station structure and policy, format—are left to their discretion, and the combinations and permutations are related to the award of a licence by the Tribunal. All who get one 'differ' from commercial stations but in how many ways depends on the dimensions of the classifying categories. In practice there is a great deal of variety (or mess) in public and in ethnic broadcasting. 'Diversity' in ethnic broadcasting means simply that it is in languages other than English. Since almost all share this characteristic, the 'diversity' is unidimensional, hence workable.

The tacit assumption about these two types of programs has been that they should be 'different' from those of commercial and national commercial services but 'not too much so'. Where they are seen as going 'outside the bounds', various kinds of trouble have followed. In the minority press in Australia, and in magazines and newsletters—which need no licence and do not usually attract any attention—there is a much wider range and much greater 'diversity'. In the minority print media there are 'extreme' elements which would never be able to secure a broadcasting licence. The Victorian Board of Jewish Deputies was genuinely startled and horrified by what it saw as anti-semitic material broadcast on 3CR, formally a commercial station with a limited licence. The same material and phrases were familiar to anyone who followed minority publications.

'Diversity' is institutionalised in the very notion of a dual system of 'sectors'—'national' and 'commercial'. The fuzzy nature of this notion is evident in the goals of the ABC—they cannot be stated in such a way that one could decide whether or not they have been met, let alone met 'properly'. (The ABC cannot be analysed in means/ends terms and economists who try to find tests of 'efficiency' for it do not grasp this.) The perennial questions about the relations of the two sectors cannot even be formulated in the crucial case where there is not a stark unidimensional dichotomy. Now that the system has four sectors or parts—commercial, national, public and SBS—most people would say it is more diverse. I believe that if diversity could be measured, which it cannot, few would want to say: 'We now have twice as much diversity, having added two new sectors.' No one knows how much 'diversity' has been added.

3. Scarcity

Scarcity of frequencies has been another rationale and apart from its regulatory function it has played a major part in Australian broadcasting history in a long and amazingly successful attempt by authorities, especially the Australian Broadcasting Control Board, to mislead people into thinking there was 'no room on the air waves'. 'Scarcity' has been used, above all, to limit the number of licences and to protect those who got them early after they were touted around by governments without many keen bidders. This is not to deny that early risk takers in radio and TV may have had an excellent case for keeping the door shut for a given time.

Diversity and scarcity in their accepted forms are now obsolescent as rationales: new technological developments—fibre optics, satellite networking, cable TV, the development of the TV set into a communication receiving and responding mechanism—will make them obsolete. Pay TV will do the rest. One will still need strict technical rules and scarcity is becoming a problem at a different level (orbital slots for satellites). But the TV system of a few stations with mass programming whose output would not become more diverse if more stations were added will not haunt policy makers and their critics for very much longer.

In Europe and Canada the state is losing control over the regulation of broadcasting within its borders. Pirates are no longer a trivial problem, though still marginal. But in many countries whole regions now can view or hear stations located abroad. These usually adopt a mode different from the state-backed local one: transborder diversity, if you like. As earth stations become cheaper, direct transmission via satellite, formerly feared by some as a major weapon of foreign governments, may become that of advertisers located abroad. In Canada the impact of US TV has now been intensified by the reception of US cable TV. This immediately multiplies the channels locally available. It has presented a serious threat to Canadian programming.

4. Public resource

The electromagnetic spectrum as a public resource and hence the claim of governments to control those who use it provide a well-worn rationale in the US. It became important since it offered a way of allowing US government intervention in the broadcasting field, circumventing the First Amendment which blocks, rather less these days it seems, legislation on the press. A government might be able to have economists give the spectrum an imputed value and then consider a lease or rental rights policy.

So far as I have been able to discover the rationale has no clear-cut legal standing here, but I am not sure. In any case it is not of political importance: students who hear about it just laugh and do not understand its relevance. In a country in which natural parks and lakes get so little protection the idea of an invisible natural public park up there in the sky, which you cannot see, smell, or inspect but in which you as a member of the public have 'rights', has no force whatever. FARB, in its commercial radio survey, asked questions about the spectrum: puzzlement and 'Reg Ansett owns it' were typical reactions.

On existing information the spectrum does not seem to offer a good rationale for regulation in Australia. Its value may be linked to scarcity notions which are becoming less relevant. What counts as a public resource is not a fact of nature, but one of social definitions. It may be worth asking whether any rights, whose rights, and what kind of rights should be linked to the spectrum.

5. Quid pro quo

The quid pro quo rationale is important but not often openly mentioned by governments. It is essentially an exchange of protection for obligations: 'As the government, directly or through a statutory corporation, we grant you a licence. We control, directly, the total number of licences. As a matter of policy we keep this at a given level. We provide for the Tribunal to consider commercial viability in issuing radio licences. Hence we erect barriers to entry into the industry. These legal barriers offer economic protection to those who are in the industry. In return for regulations which protect its stability the industry can hardly object if we attach some conditions to the licence.'

This is related to the standard Australian protection-in-return-for-concessions rationale, though there are differences. The concessions vary with the industry. The protective barriers here were for decades totally exclusive and are still so for capital city TV. But we noted that the barriers are under threat—from cable, satellites and cheap earth dishes, from a growing fragmentation of the audience or of viewers, and from the state's growing inability to stop foreign competitive messages. The quid pro quo rationale works for the industry only so long as the government freezes out competition. If it continues to do that in future it will discourage technological change and with it possible variety, diversity and alternatives. If it does not do it, or greatly weakens the protection, the industry will no longer have guaranteed stability.

One can vary the terms of the quid pro quo so that the rationale leads to different outcomes. This is a central weakness of the exchange rationale.

Conclusion

On examination, the various rationales of current policy turn out to be more vulnerable than appears at first sight, and most of them are becoming still less plausible.

All the rationales provide a vague presumption in favour of some form of government action and regulation. But some offer no clue to the type and level of regulation required, and little has been done to work out the logical implications of the others, or to define the political values—the policy assumptions—that must determine the choices.

'Impact', for example, could be made much more effective as a rationale if the would-be regulators were to finance high-quality research on the actual incidence of, say, 'harm', and invite discussion with the industry and with interested outside groups on appropriate responses to the situation as diagnosed. How far does it call for complex, externally imposed regulation, or for 'self-regulation', or for 'codes'? How far is regulation justified when the 'harm' is measured against the costs and other disadvantages of regulations? How far can industry be expected to conform to regulation when it weighs up costs and benefits? The regulators could discuss with social scientists of different methodological hues the kinds of questions that can be asked with any expectation of useful answers. As conducted at present, however, 'impact' research is of marginal use to policy makers. It is too vague, focusing too exclusively on 'harm', and not making any systematic attempt to link diagnosis with cure in the form of regulation or deregulation. This is not just a standard plea for 'more research', though that is very much needed. What I envisage here is the best kind of work, from more than one serious perspective, which relates to citizens, industry and government policy and is a critique of all of them. It must be theoretically based while aware of the severe limits to 'theory' in this field. And it should try to 'serve' yet never be a 'servant'.

Among the other rationales, it may be worth trying to impute monetary values to the 'public resource' (spectrum) and to the elements in the quid pro quo equation. Similar influence could be exercised over the fulfilment of the 'social obligation' of the media if some monetary value could be rationally attached to this obligation, or to the potentialities of controlling a licence.

The values that must be fed into all of these calculations—the definition of 'harmful effects', how much it matters if children cannot distinguish TV advertising from non-commercial content, and so on—are matters for political decision. This is where the public could have a new and positive role—in clarifying and criticising values and examining the consequences of regulation and deregulation. Citizenship would acquire significant meaning if the process were associated with genuine contributions from the policy makers in government, and was not merely an academic exercise or a public relations forum for the stations or the reformers. Temperatures on all sides would be lowered, but real outcomes would be at stake. By linking policy formulation and impact research with a learning experience for the industry and the reformers, the media field might be imbued with just a little more of the processes of reason than it has been so far.

5 Right of Reply

This previously unpublished article was a submission to an inquiry by the Australian Broadcasting Tribunal (ABT) into the Right of Reply in 1989. Although not a frequent contributor to such inquiries, Henry embraced this as an occasion to reiterate basic democratic principles, to give institutionalised recognition to the right of public participation and redress. It has a distinctively Henry emphasis: the advantages of a mix of regulation and flexibility, achieving a policy setting where the mutual rational pursuit of self-interests will work towards fruitful negotiation, and in a way that strengthens, rather than restricts, pluralism and freedom of speech.

A new standard to create the right of reply should be created. In order to combine the major advantages of regulation with those of self-regulation, and to minimise the effect that purely legal regulation would necessarily undermine immediacy in the exercise of the right, a choice of self-regulation/negotiation and of an administrative legal path should be offered.

Choice of each path has different costs and benefits. Choice would also cut resource costs to the ABT. Availability and the pattern of choices, over time, would help to evaluate the options idea and suggest whether and where else it might be taken up.

The choice option, given (but only given) a firm legal standard, would be in the enlightened self-interests of licensees and claimants to the right.

The scheme, at its most rational, also calls for a facilitator and/or a mechanical facilitating capacity. Whatever the outcome of the inquiry and the mode, if it is decided to create this new standard, TV announcements in a form and in a time zone and with a frequency approved by the ABT should be mandatory.

Background

The issue of right of reply, while immediately focused upon television, is related in complex ways to more general trends, including:

- the general growth of 'rights consciousness', in turn stimulated by social developments;
- attempts to increase the legal responsibilities of manufacturers, professionals, information gatherers and providers; and
- attempts, just beginning on the conservative side of politics in the US, to create new duties, civic obligations, for citizens, to 'counter-balance' what are seen as excessive rights claims.

The inquiry also has relevance, not yet explored, to proposed changes and opportunities in defamation laws. It occurs in the wake of the abolition of the Fairness Doctrine in the US. It seems clear that in spite of that doctrine's fate, the idea is not dead, and that, in the US, it is too early to rule out some sort of revival. On the other hand, in Australia, it is clearly not in the forefront of concerns. In our view this shows that abstract democratic principles lack linkages with institutions and organised interests. Compare the attention given, for example, to the possibility of free TV political ads where both dollars and party claims were clearly at stake.

Importance of the Issue

The key point is that while I, for one, would not have chosen 'the right of reply' as the best way of raising issues of democratic rights in the framing of television discourse, this is the framework within which I, being concerned with such issues, must now think and work.

Rejection of the right because of the difficulties of managing such a right would be a more serious blow to democratic ideas than the degree to which its acceptance will promote them in the short term. It would give the stamp of the ABT and legislative/administrative approval to the present state of affairs which limits public affairs creation, definition, selection, framing, timing, prioritisation and omission rights to owners, managers and journalists in the electronic media.

It would thus give an official stamp to the de facto exclusion of 'the public' from having a right to make an input into this sphere. Rejection hence has a major symbolic implication. It is one thing to have a given state of affairs continue because it has been, in current jargon, 'naturalised', that is, because a socially constructed arrangement has continued for so long as to seem 'natural' and the only possible one. It is quite another that, once the 'naturalised' process is scrutinised by an inquiry, it is endorsed by administrative/legal fiat. Acceptance of a new right of reply standard—if it survived the legal challenges—would:

- Affirm that in principle public affairs, controversy rights can be exercised by the 'public'.
- Permit new future remedies against what is seen as wrong/unfair to a fairly small section of 'the public'. Just as most people do not complain or protest over a wide range of things even where this is easy, except, possibly intermittently in talk, so I would not expect a flood or even a stream of right of reply demands since, at the very least, the process must be burdensome.
- Put the issue on the agenda for other related public policy issues, especially those linked to the 'information society'.

A right of reply on commercial TV would be a clear step forward in terms of a goal of wider public interest inputs. Those who genuinely accept the general idea but argue that a right of reply would have a 'chilling effect' and would restrict and narrow debate reject this. On my reading of the history of the US Fairness Doctrine I do not see any evidence that while this was in force such effects did in fact follow. Indeed since its demise, there have been claims that public issues/controversy have declined on network TV. If this is true, a lot would depend on how and for what outlets this is measured, what the contexts were and how far one can separate the Fairness Doctrine from other regulatory and deregulatory measures.

The truth is that no one can make more than an a priori general statement about chilling effects and whether they might or might not happen, and for whom. There is no way of telling. There might be, because of the right of reply, a self-imposed widening of controversial formulae. If there is no way of being reasonably certain, then one can ask where is the burden of proof? And further, might there be spin-offs from TV to increase debate in other media?

One can be sure that rejection of the right of reply standard would be a serious blow to all notions that the agendas and contents of controversies on TV are to have inputs from others than owners, managers and professionals. One can be sure that there would be some usage of the newly created right. One cannot be sure about the presence or absence of 'chilling effects' but one should assume that the vast majority of those who put forward that argument do so for other than public interest reasons.

All that can be said is that this is an open question. The uncertainty is inherent in the situation just as one can't really tell whether, given other factors, an easing of Australian defamation laws would make 'a difference' and, if so, what sort of difference in what fields. Such unavoidable uncertainty is part of many, many policy decisions. The ABT should build into any right of reply measure a regular evaluation procedure. If it is really worried about 'chill effects' it can also have a re-evaluation after a fair time span—say ten years.

I have framed this submission in terms of my concerns, that is, to increase, at minimum costs to all (including broadcasters), the possibilities of a plurality of points of view not controlled by owners, managers and professionals. It is also possible and desirable to look at the issue entirely in terms of offence and injury to individuals and groups, to perceive the issue entirely in terms of reactive redress. If the issue is framed that way the argument about 'chilling effects' would change.

The way I have framed the issue—rights of inputs to the agendas—is in conflict with a view of the issue as primarily about the standards of professionals (journalists). This apparently fair approach to the matter fails to ask who has a right to challenge these standards and to say that a given way of deciding what is and, often more importantly, what is not controversial or not worthy of serious controversy is the only one. If all journalists followed the AJA's code of ethics the issue of how key terms in it should be interpreted and by whom, and the role of non-professionals other than as passive receivers is still, for me, crucial. Moreover, ethics codes might clash with employment and career prospects.

Print vs electronic media

There is no strong tradition of 'freedom of the electronic media', nor of 'conventions as to the rights of audiences' as can be seen by different applications of the First Amendment in the US and different constitutional powers and legal controls in Australia.

Various media allow the public some capacity for input: letters to the editor, talkback radio, comments at the end of *60 Minutes* or to ABC TV's *Backchat*, SBS's *Vox Populi* and programs like the ABC's weekly *Media Watch* (which after five years has finally appeared, albeit much shrunk from its original concept). But in all of these, the final selection is made by the media organisation, and none of the TV avenues are on air, visual, or give complainants a right to frame issues their way.

Commercial TV is the most heavily consumed medium, yet the one which gives the public fewest on-air rights to participate. Every day it exercises its right to define, select and frame what is 'important' or 'controversial' or 'newsworthy' and to select, in a very brief time, something as not only a 'fact' but also as a fact with priority and authority by virtue of being on air.

The importance of the absence of viewers' rights on commercial TV is growing:

- Given its need for large audiences and its high costs TV must discriminate against non-rating less popular options.
- Cost pressures are now stronger than for a very long while—fewer risks will be taken.
- Increasing sections of the public, as 'information poor', are frozen out from current issues.

- With the wider scope of groups involved in issues and the wider range of these issues there is a greater demand for replies. This goes with the decline in the old left/right bipolar system and the rise of issues, for example, feminism, pro-market thinking, ecology and 'the greens' which cut across it.

Form and Manner

We are used to the present system and if you have spent your whole life in a country in which everything is blue the idea that some things might be yellow or green will not occur to you and, if it does, you will focus on the 'difficulties' without also looking as to what 'difficulties' are created by the all-blue system. The socially constructed patterns have been 'naturalised' and appear as obvious, self-evident, given and unchangeable. New things appear as difficult, disturbing.

There are difficulties in any new idea but they should be assessed against the difficulties of the existing scheme—as experienced by those excluded from it.

Putting the same point differently, what is a 'problem' is not self-evident but socially and culturally determined and the same holds of concepts such as 'obstacles' or 'barriers' or 'difficulties'. Thus, obviously, but insufficiently stressed, the concept of 'difficulty' must be related to what are the aims, and the importance and priority attached to them. Most of the talk about a right of reply has been in terms of how hard it would be to manage.

This is true but the importance one attaches to it must surely depend on how crucial one thinks the aim itself is. People who are pretty indifferent to this right and its implications will dwell only on the difficulties of the new. They won't admit that the existing state of affairs also has endless 'difficulties', which are hidden because they are taken for granted. Compare the endless 'difficulties' raised during the long struggles first for the vote and secondly for women having the vote. It is mindless to simply list 'difficulties' as if they were not to be evaluated against some policy goals and against the priorities different interests will attach to both.

The absence of a well resourced non-partisan pro-democratic interest group concerned with the difficulties in the existing state of affairs means that 'difficulties' usually emerge in a partisan way. The partisan makes those of his/her group visible but not those of his/her opponents. The 'difficulties' are highly differentiated and unequally distributed, and the ways to minimise and avoid them are linked in complex ways to differential resources and capacities to resist.

My sketch aims at maximising or optimising speed and hence the value of the right, and at minimising costs of the scheme for broadcasters, journalists and the ABT.

My main point is the general idea of combining a strong code with negotiation/self-regulation and giving both broadcasters and claimants incentives to avoid the necessarily inflexible legal standard.

Given—but only given—a substantive right of reply it will in most instances be in the enlightened self-interest of both broadcasters and rights claimants to choose the negotiating paths. This would give you an accountable self-regulation option backed by a standard.

The claimant wants, in nearly all cases, one thing above all, which legal regulation cannot give him or her: speed, immediacy. Given appeals, delays are not avoidable. There seems no way to have only a legal path and avoid delays. (If only a legal path is possible, I'd have to support that but with great reservations.)

The major negotiable resources and claims are: speed, length, placement, frequency, production costs and effects on ratings at the time and on the 'flow' of the evening etc.

Broadcasters do not want a right of reply at all and will fight it to the highest courts. (Alas, they are not likely to agree that a properly mounted 'Right of Reply' show drama could be high rating, dramatic and rushed by advertisers.) If broadcasters have to have a right of reply at all, they will want as much control as they can, over who is to get it, how soon, where, how often, at what costs and over how supposed damage to ratings and costs might be minimised. Rights claimants in most cases will want top speed, prime time, greater length/frequency and attractive (hence costly) production values. Given a right of reply standard, claimants and broadcasters should have the choice of making trade-offs which may differ from case to case, for example, speed vs placement, length vs production values.

'Immediacy' is the most important and valuable resource for both: it increases drama and hence impact, makes the issue more memorable, has a better chance of making sense without longish explanations.

In this scheme you need someone who is easily accessible, available to help with the choice and as neutral as possible. That is the facilitator whose main job it is to:

- be announced on TV in a form and at times and frequency determined by the ABT;
- be available as a recorded agreed-on pros/cons message; and
- answer all queries, with all conversations recorded.

His/her main job is to stress the dual paths idea and make it clear that both have their own costs and benefits.

People and groups who enter either path might surrender their right to sue for defamation (as is done by the Press Council).

Other Issues

I am not 'ducking' any of the issues because I am sure that if there is a choice the overwhelming proportion of issues will be settled by negotiation. If this fails the option is the long, expensive, clumsy, subject-to-appeals legal path. Stations have an interest to avoid costs and delays and save the resources in executive time consumed. Hence I have not, deliberately, worked out a scheme which relies on legal/administrative standards only.

But some comments seem indicated.

1. Who is to define the key terms 'directly', 'affected', 'person', 'group', 'controversial issues', 'public importance'? The ABT has to do this but should do so through public consultation once the right of reply has been accepted in principle.

2. Which group? If there is more than one claimant, which? One can look at representativeness, for example, the Directory of Australian Associations has membership figures but are these audited? One can look at 'first come first served' or, very Australian, draw lots.

3. Time: The standard must specify the time zones for the

reply which might be within X per cent of the original telecast. Negotiations can trade this off for something else.

4. Exclusions: This is the toughest of the lot—should anyone be excluded from claiming a right? If so, on what grounds? The fears that (say) alleged child molesters might wish to defend their rights to molest are, while not silly, probably vastly exaggerated. If one combines an approach in terms of known support numbers, plus public policy issues, plus ABT standards, some of these fears disappear. If the scheme re alternative paths is adopted broadcasters could insist on not offering the negotiation path. But this remains a serious issue for anyone concerned with a clash of principles.

I have no submission on this point since I have been thinking about it in other contexts for some years without coming to a clear and context-less conclusion. Even if public policy excludes some there might be others one would feel most uncomfortable about if let in and of course public policy itself must be subject to criticism. Simple minded dogmatists have no problems, others must.

5. Inequalities: It has been said repeatedly that such a right will give more to the powerful and resource rich than to the isolated, powerless and resource poor.

- This is true, and means no more than that the powers of the ABT to change the social structure, even if it wished to have them, are very limited.
- It does not mean that the hitherto excluded will not get some additional rights.
- The ABT can to some extent equalise access and availability if the rights are publicised in the way suggested.

6. Facts/opinions: A division of standards has been suggested. But current theories in the philosophy of the social sciences do not allow for a self-evident notion of 'fact' outside a theory/paradigm framework. True there is consensus in some cases that X is a 'fact' but those are not likely to come up. Who'd decide 'the facts' about kangaroo cullings, unemployment, the debt burden, the categorisation of migrants? Agreed-on 'facts' are most unlikely to come into play (except maybe on wrong names and dates); for the rest the issue will be con-

tested, that is, how far is it a matter of opinion as to what 'the facts' are?

7. Costs: If this is linked to giving citizenship a better chance, commercial TV can, given the social nature of the licence, bear some burdens, but since the aim is related to a more rational and less unilateral broadcasting structure, not all. I would favour some nominal access fee for rights claimants if public policy allows this. It would be similar to entry fees/deposits and help to screen out some not serious. The usual exemptions (for example, legal aid provisions) for resourceless parties can be made.

I have focused entirely on the group rights issue and tackled that in the light of what I see as the promotion of the public interest while minimising frictions and costs and, crucially, offering both broadcasters and right demanders choices which enable them to behave more rationally through an appeal to their longer range enlightened self-interests.

I am not 'in principle' for or against regulation or deregulation and have hence combined elements from both because in this case—given the value of immediacy—a strong case for offering flexibility in return for speed exists. For another case I might prefer a different mix.

I very rarely make submissions since I wish to be able to talk to a wide range of interests, often conflicting, without being 'tagged' so as to maximise my life work's goal: to attempt to get interests to fight out their conflicts in a more rational way so as to increase intelligent and self-critical plurality in society and do so with an appeal, not to the intellect alone, but to enlightened self-interest.

I stress that the key point is the mix of self-legal regulation and the facilitation element.

6 Censorship: Trends and Paradoxes

Anti-censorship was a cause close to Henry's heart; the column that he wrote in the Australian *until 1975 was titled 'Speaking Freely'. This chapter was delivered to a seminar organised by the Australian National Commission for UNESCO on Entertainment and Society in 1978. As one would expect, it has a vigorous critique of the authoritarianism and anti-intellectualism of the Festival of Light, one unintended consequence of which was to make it more difficult for anyone wanting to mount a more rational argument for censorship. Less predictably, it then discusses the value-laden conceptualisations sometimes masking the similarities between official interventions encouraging and discouraging types of cultural products, considers how feminist critiques have brought new intellectual force to debates over censorship, and how under new media scholarship the framing of the debate around single obscene or violent passages may need to change to the long term impacts of whole genres.*

We are a very long way from the old clichés about censorship—from the battles of yesteryear in which quite a few people saw censorship as stemming some tide they feared might engulf civilisation and corrupt youth, while others thought that only when the last censor was hanged by the entrails of the last professional decency-monger would true and unfettered creative freedom flourish.

Note how scattered the whole enterprise now is, and how restricted the functions of the Film Censorship Board are. It is not—except for certain film advertisements—concerned with printed matter. Most of us would not be able to say who, if anyone, was so concerned and precisely what de jure authority and de facto powers they might retain. The key task of the board is that of classification. Straight out bans happen, but they are now rare and disputes over them die down quickly.

The classification job, however, is further restricted. Only the 'R' category has legal force but, and this is a key point, the board has not got the nasty job of enforcing or purporting to enforce the implementation of the 'R' age restrictions. That is not its task and thus it is not officially concerned with the matter.

I doubt whether there are any serious studies about the effectiveness of the implementation of the 'R' classifications, any more than there are good surveys on the attempt to relate the sale of alcohol to age. One's a priori assumption, in both cases, is that the law constitutes some kind of barrier which has more than a purely symbolic meaning but that real enforcement would require a gigantic and expensive apparatus plus compulsory identification cards of some kind. It is significant that not even the famous fighter against filth, the Reverend Fred Nile of the Festival of Light, has much to say on this issue.

The classifications used by the Film Censorship Board and the notions behind them—the assumption that there can be any rational basis or bases for such classifications—do raise general issues. But these are hardly discussed. The reason is clear enough: even the 101 per cent libertarians who oppose all classifications don't find many cases in the film field where they can see the issue as one of importance. They prefer not to become involved in the defence of fifth-rate cheap muck (often more ludicrous and boring than nasty), even though in principle they would defend the rights of the muck merchants.

The Festival of Light

What of the more general discussion of pornography, media, censorship? In Australia no serious case has been put for censorship for a long while. In the last few decades, the only person I know who attempted this for a while was Peter Coleman, Liberal MLA in New South Wales. He also, mainly in *Quadrant*, reprinted some of the more serious US contributions on the pornography-censorship theme. Coleman got very little change out of this, and his highly intelligent and sophisticated presentation fell flat.

It is deplorable that the Festival of Light is the only group which now regularly and publicly concerns itself with censorship issues. It prefers the label 'quality control' as if cultural products were homogeneous and as if there were a good deal of consensus about the criteria by which they and their effects should and could be judged. This assumption shows what is wrong with the Festival: it does not and cannot realise and admit that there is a genuine and proper dispute about what is and is not 'poisonous' about cultural products in a way in which there is not about, say, meat. There is no complete consensus about meat and, if vegetarians and alternative lifestyle people become more powerful, the existing degree of consensus must decline. But, with meat, there is a widespread consensus about what is 'quality', and what are 'bad effects on health' and about the methods by which such effects can be appraised.

What can and must be said about the Festival of Light in relation to censorship issues?

1. First and foremost, the group has benefited from skilful public relations.

2. It is widely feared. Its flamboyant presentations and methods give it a prominence and irritation value that the nature of its dogmatic assertions does not merit.

3. The Festival is widely taken, by young and eager students and many others, as the chief symbol of the censor. Since it is easy to hate (and, for its supporters, clearly easy to love), it has become the favourite thing to kick around when there is any concern with censorship. (A single good study of the totally non-hateable, non-visible, non-dramatic firm of Gordon and Gotch and its position in the distribution system would be of much greater value than yet another attack on the Festival.)

4. Some of the concerns put forward in an objectionable and indefensible manner by the Festival of Light are, in and by themselves, worth serious attention.

Thus the issue of exploitation and manipulation in films, the question of how far what kind of producers prey on what sort of needs and how far they manage to create or at least shape wants and preferences is a very serious and major issue. It is major because the same question can and should be asked over a wide range of enterprises from advertising via TV, the new feminism or gay liberation to the Young Liberals, defence policy, and the images many trade union leaders create about employers and many employers create about trade unions and their leaders. It is also a perfectly serious concern if we look at the notion of a cultural racket and then apply this to both mainstream and alternative cultures.

Another issue which over time has been raised by the Festival is sadism and its possible links with pornography. Again, by itself and as such, it is an important and serious issue. The broader issue of violence, its definition, its impact via TV on viewers and more especially on children is perhaps in recent years the most carefully and widely researched field in the US and there is a plethora of very good studies (Comstock 1975; Murray 1977).

The Festival has also, at times, sounded somewhat similar to the Women's Liberation Movement it otherwise utterly condemns, through its references to the pornographer as the exploiter of women, who are presented purely as objects of sexual gratification.

Yet, sadly, it is probably the case that the way the Festival presents its assertions—it is not given to serious arguments and, in spite of a pretence to the contrary, is deeply hostile to empirical research except where it believes such favours its cause—and its mode of conducting its campaigns does great harm to any serious discussions of such issues.

The Festival intends to foster concern with such issues and to promote 'quality control'. What it helps to achieve is the damping down of serious debate. The activities of the Festival unintentionally tend to protect if not foster the very things it believes it is fighting. In this sense, carefully spelled out as above, one can, if one sees the need to be dramatic, assert that the intentions of the Festival, to put down pornography and sleazy works, are unrelated to the outcome or consequences of its activities which help to protect pornography and sleaziness.

It hardly needs stressing but should be said for the record that the distinction between intentions and consequences or results is a general one. Of course it is not in any sense being implied that the Festival or the people who agree with it would share my judgment.

If there were an organisation with concerns about sadism,

sexploitation, cultural racketeering and so on that operated with a totally different style from that of the Festival and, most importantly, that was willing to make distinctions which the Festival with its sledgehammer techniques refuses to make, it might well get support from some academics and intellectuals.

As it is, we have the deplorable state of affairs that, on the one hand, the Festival raises some important issues; on the other hand the way they are raised, looked at, and publicised (plus the fact that the Festival also deals with a large number of phoney issues) makes it impossible for most thinking people to be in any way associated with it. (What I say now does not apply or applies only with serious qualifications to the work of the one academic who works with the Festival—Dr John Court of Flinders University.)

In general the Festival style and methods are crude, tend to be semi-literate, are bucolic, label and smear opponents as lustful, hedonistic, materialistic and probably communist or communist influenced. On top of that the Festival engages in attacks on minorities, especially homosexuals; assumes quite falsely that its standards are those of the community rather than those of one strand in it; and falsely presents itself as representing the whole spectrum of Christianity. It harangues people and its claims put off many who might otherwise have some concern with some of the issues it raises.

Changes

In what I have said so far there is a tacit inference that issues about control and censorship, though they seem no longer of any great weight, are with us for a very long time yet. This indeed, is my view: the assumption that some processes and events need control and—a different assumption which by no means follows—that such control is to be exercised by and through some official body is not one I can see vanishing for a long time yet.

The demand for control and maybe for censorship as a mechanism of control is a function of psychological and symbolic 'needs' as well as of conflicting views as to moral and ethical standards and as to the nature of morality itself. Different, often quite vague and tacitly held assumptions as to the relation between law and morality and as to the cost/benefit side of legal controls are also involved.

It is possible that people will increasingly believe in controls or new controls but be less and less happy about a board or committee to exercise and administer them. There is some evidence, fragmentary as yet, that there may be a shift from official control mechanisms to vigilante-like unofficial ones, tied to some interest group or social movement. It is too early to say much more on this point.

What other changes are there in this field? First, if it is true that we are at the beginning of or already somewhat advanced in a process labelled 'the decline of capitalism', or if a lot of people believe we are there, then there will be a desperate search for gimmicks and fixits to stem what to those who support the system is a deplorable process of decay, a slide towards something more nefarious. If so, there will be an increasing demand for tighter and more efficient screws, 'backlash' if you like.

The only comment I wish to make about this is that the process is one of hit-and-miss fears: the Festival of Light people and, alas, many of its small 'l' liberal opponents of a humanist bent, talk and write as if there were some solid knowledge of the causes of decay, and as if one could identify 'decay' in a society the same way one can identify it in a tooth.

But this is not so. Even if we agree on what the criteria of decay are, its causes, either in a given period or over the history of peoples, are very hard to find. It is also an absurdly simplistic and naive view that if you did find them, you could therefore somehow reverse and fix them.

The second change is more interesting—it can be labelled as a concern with events changing into one with processes. This may be part and parcel of the partial reaction, in some quarters, against specialisation and fragmentation and the search for some kind of over-arching 'meaningful' interpretation of social life.

The symbolic scissors of the censor cut out particular events, single scenes or shots, whether these extend over time or not. Yet while the critique of sexism and racism is also concerned with taking particular events as especially offensive and objectionable, it puts more and more stress on the whole process, especially on the daily and 'commonsense' habits and routines that lead to and produce the events. The same kind of stress on the normal, habitual, regular process of decision making as to what to define as newsworthy and what sort of people to approach for comments, which in turn reinforce these kinds of decisions and are taken as evidence that they are 'right', can be seen in more recent studies of media and of the fashioning of news.

The cruder and more simplistic focus on events is still at the centre of many an argument. It is a convenient way for the censor to operate: if processes are to be tackled, then many films would have to be eliminated in their entirety rather than cut just a bit or 'reconstructed'.

Yet, for instance, in the work of George Gerbner on violence on TV, a concentration on drip-drip-drip processes rather than on the particular events from which they are made up permits an important focus on cumulative, latent, and long-range effects. It also opens the door to the study of the contexts within which media operate and are perceived. If this approach spreads, then the whole idea of what it means to censor may change: there may have to be concern with much more that is implicit and indirect. Clearly, even if a board were enlarged and the status and education of the people on it were raised considerably, a stress on process would be an administrative nightmare since the consensus as to meaning would decline.

The third change one might briefly mention concerns the very conception of censorship itself. I have already speculated about the possible shift from the official to the unofficial. But the more general point is that there are a great variety of possible controls, and a great many ways of trying to work them out. Only some are considered to be censorship. Yet it may be increasingly important to look at the whole range and ask ourselves how far a number of things are the functional equivalent of what either the new or the old 'proper' censorship boards do or did.

One instance must suffice: we have had attempts in Australia, going back at least to the Bruce-Page period of the late 1920s, to get governments to support the Australian film industry and, over time, to bolster the employment of Australian actors in films, plays and TV productions with Australian content.

The main (not the only) definition of 'Australian content' has been in terms of the number and type of Australians employed on various levels or in given types of positions. The defence of such measures has always been in some kind of cultural terms—retaining 'our' heritage, displaying 'our' way of life, being independent and not dominated by others of given nationalities, either multinational or transnational.

While there is an endless debate over issues of this kind, it is cast usually in economic terms: one side says that they are all for Australian content but are in the TV, radio, or film business to make money. They can afford, we are told, only a given percentage of the more expensive local product, and economies of scale make them opt, with regret, for the much cheaper US-produced one.

The fact is that the government, if it intervenes at all, fosters a given cultural product and excludes another overseas-produced one or cuts down its use. In the recent debates about an international 'free flow' of news and information the plainly political issues have been spelled out clearly. But in Australia the tariff or the points system or the quota systems which can alter the structure of what we are likely to encounter on television are not perceived by more than a very few as having (with a different label) partly similar functions as the censor.

I am not here asserting, let alone arguing, that they do. All I wish to stress is that we are all exposed to and put up with a great variety of controls with very different reactions and that one of the reasons is that we see one type as censorship control while we may look at another with partly similar functions as the creation of employment opportunities for Australians and/or the promotion of Australian culture.

Conclusion

To summarise: I have sketched a few ideas for discussion. On none of them have I done more than throw out a few hints about some of the points one would have to consider in a more thorough argument.

1. Issues about censorship and control seem to have

become unfashionable and marginal. This is a superficial conclusion. Rather they may well assert themselves in relatively new and different ways, and there may be unofficial but powerful control mechanisms.

2. The present structure is overall (taking the printed and the audio and visual media) not easily characterised. There is a fair bit of symbolism with no agreed-on follow-through or enforcement and this state of affairs is by no means to be automatically deplored.

3. There is no serious argument from those who wish for controls or more controls. The main group is the Festival of Light, which has received undue attention and which also unintentionally makes it difficult for intellectuals to discuss serious issues as to violence, sadism and the effects of TV and films.

4. Any proper discussion would have to look at the whole range of controls, and ask why some are labelled 'censorship' or 'classification' while others are not seen as such. How far do controls with very different labels and images have roughly similar functions? If they do, does this matter and should we look at the functions once more?

7 The Morality of Political Advertising

This chapter is based upon an address Henry gave to an audience of advertising executives after the 1980 federal election. His mocking tone about when advertising people worry about morality gives way to a searching consideration of the epistemological and enforcement difficulties of superficially desirable ideas about ethical standards in political advertising.

Typically, where there is little dough, there is lots of worry about ethics. If the Australian Democrats have an agency that gets paid, maybe it would worry. But you can bet that the agencies telling us about the Liberal heaven and Labor hell, or the Labor heaven and Liberal hell, never worry about the ethics of political advertising.

Sure, if the agencies for the big battalions were cornered, they might produce some choice phrases of deep concern. Their clients are parties. Parties are not supposed to openly sell policies like others sell soap. Parties are political entrepreneurs, partly involved with ethical and moral phrases and policies which are supposed to be linked to 'vision' and other semi-tangibles. They must claim to be upright.

Yet, the truth is not hard to find. Political advertising is one of those topics which is in the grab bag of the AFA and AANA and of nearly all individual agencies under 'other'.

Evidence? No, no survey. You can look for evidence in action: How much do trade associations bother and what do they bother about? If they bother, then someone, somewhere, worries that the subject is, or is about to become, an 'issue'. Any 'issue' can rock the boat. Where you have issues, you have those mind-boggling, mouth-watering, splendidly crafted, self-regulation codes. You and I know that we all spend many days a year admiring the skill, thought and finesse of those documents and the tender care lavished on the codes. As we savour the codes, we know that all is well in the industry.

There is no code of self-regulation for political advertising—a sure sign that it is one of those topics mainly fit for students' essays, Sunday sermons on social responsibility in our decaying society, and parties such as the Australian Democrats far removed from power.

That may not continue forever. If there is public funding of parties, there might be an attempt to check on what sorts of whoppers they tell with our money. And in the US where there is political funding, you get complicated proposals on codes for paid political TV.

True, now and then, the cry goes out that the government should apply the standards it applies to others to itself. As we shall see, this won't work. It's not a case of double standards; rather I shall argue that the idea of moral standards applied to political action, or policies and advertisements about them, won't wash.

As with all lobbyists, what the industry advocates proclaim in public and what the individuals who work in the industry privately are concerned about, are two different things. There are a very few people in advertising who worry about the ethics of political ads—Phillip Adams, atypical in so many ways, comes to mind. There are a few more who think that political advertising is a bad thing since it brings advertising, as a whole, into disrepute. They are opposed to it, or at least critical of it, on prudential grounds. And there are some who want longer and (they hope) more rational political ads. But, taken all together, it's a fair guess—I have no hard data—that we are talking of a handful of people.

Why is this so? All criticism of advertising, which is not merely a general criticism of capitalism (some is—though much less than the official industry line proclaims), works with concepts such as 'harm' and makes assumptions about a causal link between a given type of advertising and 'harm'.

Take the smoking case.[1] I am not concerned here with 'the facts', only beliefs about 'facts'. I have no empirical evidence that my beliefs about industry beliefs are true. My views could not be checked by survey.

But if you have not met many people in agencies or client companies who are unhappy about smoking and advertising, it would be strange. Few can afford to say so in public. Why so much uneasiness in the commercial world then?

Consider what is involved:

- there is a relatively clear concept of 'harm';
- there is a more than normal degree of consensus on its boundaries;
- there is a widespread and well-supported belief that smoking is causally responsible for that harm;
- there is a widespread belief, probably more widespread outside the industry than inside it, that advertising is directly and causally linked with more than the distribution of brand shares. Many believe it is a major force in young people taking up smoking.

The industry, in its defence, naturally and inevitably, focuses on the complexities of causation, on the multiplicity of factors besides advertising which might be involved. It uses a model of scientific evidence and scientific proof, by now highly contested amongst social scientists but still accepted by many and which, of course, yields a verdict of 'not proven'.

It is not hard to meet advertising people at all levels who don't agree with the official industry line and would like to see all smoking ads banned if (it is, to be sure, a crucial 'if') they could feel sure that this ban would not spread. The industry lobbyists, doing their job well, argue that, if you give in on A you must give in on B and so on down the slippery slope. (Dogmatically I will just say that the slippery slope argument cannot be tested in a general way. Sometimes, indeed, the slope is slippery; at other times it is not.)

Reverting to politics:

- There is no consensus on what would be politically harmful.
- There is some broad agreement amongst academics and non-academics who have reflected at some length on the issue as to what is wrong with political advertising. But it is a very vague consensus, and not as specific in content nor as widespread as in the case of smoking.
- There is very little evidence of a scientific kind—by the standards of 'science' used in the smoking controversy—which

links irrational political advertising with irrational political decision making.

What are the main worries about political advertising?:

- Political decisions ought to be made in the light of a serious examination of policies and issues. Political advertising must downplay both. If it deals with policies and issues, it must grossly distort them since it must oversimplify them.
- Political decisions are important and serious in a way a decision on which brand of soap to buy is not.
- If we compare the content of most political advertising with that of a good deal of non-political advertising, we find that the political stuff is specially dishonest and unfair.

It's this point which worries some in the industry. The industry has, for decades, helped to support government action against fly-by-night shonky firms. They, of course, argued about what and who falls into this group. But the general argument—that advertising is a good, decent and worthy enterprise which cannot tolerate plain fraud since it brings the industry into disrepute and might lead to the regulation of those who are 'good'—has been accepted very widely.

For quite a few, political advertising falls by definition into the category of the fraudulent and highly deceptive. Hence, unless controlled or banned, it will affect the standing, credibility and level of regulation of the whole industry. This argument—'Never mind whether political advertising is ethical or not, to tolerate it is simply bad business and, if its control or elimination goes with a better ethical stance, fine'—is, perhaps, the most popular.

- If we could control the content of political ads so that we get fewer lies, or if we could make them longer and more thoughtful, we would enhance the rationality of voters.

Duping the voters

The final scene of the 1970s film *The Candidate*, where a professional manager fashions a successful campaign around an attractive young social activist, expresses the central fears of the critics of political advertising: that a 'product' can be packaged and sold to an unsophisticated electorate just like soap or toothpaste. The victorious candidate anxiously ponders whether he is actually qualified for public office. He turns to his campaign manager, a hired gun already looking for new faces to sell, and says: 'But what do we do now?'

A recent work by advertising man Robert Spero, *The Duping of the American Voter: Dishonesty and Deception in Presidential Television Advertising*, focuses upon TV campaign commercials, and argues they are chock-full of political claims so fraudulent that networks and government would have banned them had cornflakes or soap been involved. Spero writes: 'The First Amendment (which guarantees freedom of the press) has never been so corrupted. It has been made a smoke screen behind which the unscrupulous candidate can confidently shout "fire!" in the crowded nation without fear of penalty and with high office the all too frequent reward.'

About three-quarters of the book is an historical attack on such commercials, from Eisenhower in 1952 to the Jimmy Carter and Gerald Ford spots in 1976. The material is useful. The typically American attempt to rate all of them against eighteen standards used by the National Broadcasting Company (NBC) to screen non-political advertising is, at first, suggestive but gets tedious pretty fast. Yes, you've guessed it: Spero finds lots of 'violations' in every advertisement. He takes a 60 second Carter commercial of four years ago and finds all these remarks by Carter 'deceptive, misleading and unfair claims': 'I started my own campaign . . . I didn't have any political organisation. Not much money . . . Nobody knew who I was . . . To special interest groups I owe nothing.'

It never occurs to him that the use of the NBC code to test political commercials begs the central question raised here: Are criteria, which may make sense in one field, also reasonably applicable to political matters?

Political advertising by its very nature in a party system must knock the other side. But, unlike most other comparative advertising, it deals only to a limited extent with hard data.

In politics it is not possible to find out 'the truth' about what will work as a policy. It is easier to get some agreement on what won't work. Experts who are as detached as possible can find some consensus over a range of alleged remedies and agree that these are all snake oil. But, even if that is so, it does not help much: politics is not, in any sense, a science nor can policies be scientific. The experts may all be wrong and a discredited policy yet prove a winner while defying analysis as to why that's so.

More importantly, there can be expertise in working out social costs and benefits, but the idea of an 'expert' on priorities, compromises and clashes of value is inherently absurd. How trade-offs should be made, how often, at whose expense and over what period are matters of conflicting interests and values linked to them in complex ways.

It is possible to say that a political advertisement lies about a given statistic if the two sides agree about the basis of the statistical data and the expression of it. It is possible to find lies about 'hard facts'. However, these are mostly of little interest or importance. To acquire meaning they need context, which cannot be 'hard'.

The idea of political deception is much less simple than that of deception in many other fields. Look back at the Carter commercial: each key word is vague and subject to endless disputes. 'My own' is vague, as is 'political organisation'. How much money is 'not much money'? When we say 'nobody knew who I was' we do not normally mean 'nobody at all'. But how many people must know who you are before it becomes deceptive to say 'nobody knows'? When does one 'owe' something to an interest group? And what sort of obligation is meant?

If you found a way to make all political advertising rational and accurate, or even if you improved its rationality and accuracy greatly, what would you have to do? And what would follow?

You would have to *eliminate politics as we know it.*

You would have to cut out all slogans, mood pieces and jingles. You'd have to cut out references to trust, leadership, loyalty, fear, conflict, commitment, solidarity, envy. You'd have to chop appeals to justice and equity, as well as those to greed, competition and enterprise.

You could not 'Raise the Standard' or 'Turn on the Lights' or follow 'The Light on the Hill'. You'd not be allowed to say that Liberals are in the 'lead' without specifying where they are leading us and at what cost to whom. There could be no 'Hamer makes it Happen' without a long and detailed analysis of what 'it' was, what its costs were, over what time and by what standards and on and on. Indeed, many academic political analysts, if they were forced to conduct this sort of enterprise, would claim that no politician can ever 'make' anything happen. They think that the causal links between political actions and outcomes are rarely known.

Advertisements would have to be huge books with many contexts and all sorts of if/then scenarios. The most obvious thing about current political advertisements and promises is that they are not usually stated (where sufficiently specific so that one could, in principle, decide whether they'd been broken) with any conditions attached to them. But, of course, the elbow room that an Australian government of any colour has depends only to a small part on its own efforts, intelligence and drive. To a very large extent—how large is an issue in dispute—we are at the mercy of world economic forces which we do not control.

So a truthful and accurate advertisement would be a monster in length, complexity and contingencies. And once you'd attempted to truthfully specify even a wide, let alone a 'complete' range, of circumstances, you could employ the total bureaucracy, computerise your inputs and still get nowhere. This means that, if one could reach agreement on truth in political advertisement and in politics, the already low interest in politics would decline sharply and apathy further increase. It is not reasonable to swamp voters with a sea of information in which they will sink rather than swim.

Moreover, the more truthful and reasonable the political material, the less enthusiasm and commitment to a given party it would evoke. A policy would have to be presented as not so very different from that of your opponents after all. You'd have to point out that both your party and theirs had lots of poor, some mediocre, and a few good people and ideas. You could say little more than that your party would try hard (as would theirs) and that most things you tried out, if you got to power, would not work, or would work imperfectly, or would have unforeseen consequences, and that all this would also be true of your opponents.

How many people would march behind a pale, highly

qualified, most imperfectly crafted banner of truth, the only huge letters on it being 'fallibility'?

I am unimpressed by the people who don't mind political advertisements as such, but simply want them longer. Somehow a 60 second job or a two minute one is supposed to take care of 'complexity' and allow calmer reflection. Nonsense.

A 'political fact bank'?

Let's get back to Robert Spero's *Duping of the American Voter.* He believes that deceptive political advertising made a major difference to the fate of the US and of the world. He sees the television attack on Barry Goldwater as a warmonger as 'unfair and largely unwarranted'. Without it, he argues, Lyndon Johnson would have won by a much narrower margin in 1964. Had this happened he 'might well have persuaded himself to hesitate in going ahead with his Vietnam adventure'. Note how, from a simple point, we move rapidly into the field of complete speculation. If there is good evidence on how political margins affect presidential risk-taking, I do not know of it.

Spero would like to ban political TV commercials, but admits that would not work and would be unconstitutional in the US. Nor can they, given the First Amendment, be censored. What then?

You've guessed it: he's got a code of standards which creates many possible offences. Who would check and enforce it? A vague 'administrative group' would detect and publicise violations. By what standard would these people work?

You've guessed it once more: we are, after all, in the 1980s and databanks must come to the rescue. We'd have a 'Political Fact Bank' with computerised information about the candidates and their records supplemented by 'non-partisan' statistics on areas such as the impact of tax relief and armament sufficiency.

It is not clear just what force there would be behind those standards except publicity. One assumes that, if you have been found guilty of a code violation, you will correct the offending material or lose votes. The composition of the 'administrative group' would be all-important—well, yes, who has not dreamed, now and then, of playing God—but pretty soon all its members would beg for rapid euthanasia.

Conclusion

To summarise: political advertising is necessarily full of deception, half-truths, exaggerations and falsities. It is that way because all forms of politics are that way, but political lies are not like lies about soap or cornflakes. Politics does not deal with 'products' which can be checked and evaluated in the way a car can be, provided that car has only one clear function.

If worried enough to care, you can compare brands of soap or toothpaste in terms of some hard criteria. But there is no possible way you can compare soft appeals which rely on fantasy, pride, ego-boosting, fear, or alienation. You could, if it is important, have an enforceable code for cosmetics. But it could only deal with clear-cut harms to the skin and pharmaceutical properties. No code can deal with the key content of most cosmetics advertisements which deal in intangibles.

Politics deals both with tangibles and symbols. One could—it would be one of my bottom priorities—work for years and dig out a code of 'political facts'. But that would be very narrow and have no contextual meaning. You can work out objectively how many houses were built by the government in period Y provided you agree on what counts as a 'house' and what as a 'building'. But what that means in a given context and whether it was a good or bad thing to build those houses must be subject to subjective political argument, and no code or law can tell you in what context you ought to consider that issue as against some other.

Truth is hardly ever simple or short in politics. Truthful political promotion would have to stress context and complexity and imperfection to such a degree as to bore the pants of most men and women and send them to sleep.

News

8 Images of Politics in the Press

Henry had an early and enduring interest in public images of politicians and leaders (for example, Mayer, Loveday and Westerway, 1960; Mayer and Curnow 1968). This chapter, originally commissioned by the Australian Journalism Review, *is a revealing critique of the tacit imagery and problematic assumptions underlying apparently 'hard' news reporting—ideas of leadership, motivation, the framing of issues, the implications of labels unthinkingly applied.*

How do Australian papers with some ambition treat politics? What tacit assumptions about the nature of politics and politicians are covered by the existing hard news formula?

This exercise in speculation—it is no more—glances at these issues. It neither comments on downmarket papers nor looks at why news formulas are as it takes them to be. Suffice it to stress that they are not a simple reflection of a social system, nor of structural elements (classes, elites, interest groups, corporations) within it. Nor do they interact with their sources and with (parts of) the system in clearly predictable ways.

Journalism is, in one sense as a regular activity, 'about' the reduction of uncertainty and the production of material fed into a very visibility-constraining apparatus of production. But the fascination it has for both its practitioners and its analysts arises from the inherent conflicts between 'information' and 'entertainment' aspects and from the elements of creativity, contingency, messiness, and quirkiness found in it. These exist to a degree and with a scope only discernible through very tedious, lengthy, subtle, empirically based (but not empiricist) study in all social systems. Even in those countries where there seems to be a simple, clear-cut and severely sanctioned set of norms for the media, we know little about how far the element of contingency (as against some organisational/bureaucratic and structural model) goes. How does it differ within and between countries and within and between kinds of media?

Hard news

The starting point has been repeated endlessly: hard news can't handle process, is reductionist and treats events and politics in an ahistorical way, as a glut of occurrences. It cannot cope with any long-run historical processes, nor with complexity.

This, of course, is 'our' view of what is 'hard'. The Cuban or Nigerian views, for example, are very different. 'Hard', 'soft' and similar news categories are themselves cultural artefacts. The astonishment that another news system does not report, say, disasters is itself cultural.

Two aspects of hard news have been less commented on. It cannot deal with the fact that what is and is not 'politics' is itself a contested notion. Long before the rise of feminism, the New Left of the 1960s or even the working class or bourgeoisie, the boundaries of 'the political' were fought over. Hard news concentrates on what many political analysts have also focused on: a regular, easily located, clearly identified and institutionalised 'politics'. Journalistic skills in hard news are displayed at their best in short bursts of intensity during which the overall notion of what is and what is not a story has become ritualised but which yet leaves room for angles and surprises often created by individuals. Elections fit this bill.

Hard news is not able to spell out, except in empty formulas ('dependence on the US economy') the ways in which external constraints, Australia's part in 'the world system', limit the elbow room for internal politics. The few journalists on the left make dependency central but in a formalist stereotype ('a lapdog of US imperialism') and mainly in order to protest against it. 'Dependency' should be overcome so that Australia's 'autonomy' (a concept that evokes many of the feelings which nationalism does, but in a less openly ideological way) might flourish. There are few even semi-serious attempts at working out the scenarios which might yield different degrees of autonomy in various fields so that one might think differently of, say, culture as compared with technology or the economy.

Hard news constraints squeeze social and political life into a procrustean mould.

Motives

The most obvious way journalists do this is in their reductionist pop psychology. Why do some people go into politics and stay there? Hard news operates with an apparently knowing and supposedly no-nonsense but in fact infantile, non-discriminating and indefensible notion of politics as the realm of the most naked and visible self. It not only makes selfishness the central notion but also uses a very narrow concept of self-interest. It tries to 'explain' all actions whether being interested in politics, standing for pre-selection, forming a new party, or running a faction, in terms of a self-centred drive for perks and power.

'Self' is a concept which can bear any weight you give it, depending entirely on how one thinks of and conceptualises that self. The Australian press's concept tends to be so narrow that it even has trouble in handling enlightened self-interest. It is happiest and most comfortable when it can point to some 'perk' or 'privilege' supposed to motivate politicians. It tries to handle longer-range aims mainly by claiming that the carrot is still dangling there for all to see. The person concerned is merely waiting for a better opportunity to take a major bite at it.

Treatment of 'perks'—a marvellous, sharp, brief, journalistic headline word—also illustrates the point. It often extends from politicians to public service 'fat cats'. Often perks are very petty or have long been enjoyed by private enterprise employees. The link between self and some marginal perk becomes then more obviously absurd. But politicians and public servants by definition can't win: the more marginal the perk the greedier, the more ruthlessly amoralistically self-interested they can be pictured as or tacitly inferred to be.

Take the accounts of income and salary cuts often attached to taking on some high office in a statutory authority, the public service or the judicial sphere. The press must hint that people who switch from lucrative private practice to the less lucrative public sphere are no good, or that they compensate for the drop in income by being able to expand the scope for their egos.

This fits in well with images of politicians or bureaucrats as puritanical, interventionist, power-crazy, potentially coercive busybodies and zealots who stroke their self only if and when they can pass another law or make up another interfering and unnecessary regulation.

Where this approach does not work at all, the press is puzzled. It cannot handle complexity within the hard news notion of self as purely determined by narrow notions of prestige, status and power.

Of course, to develop this point, one would have to look at what is supposed to drive businesspeople. And, at length, one would have to bring out the gender-bound nature of news concepts and look at such issues from a feminist perspective.

Principles

Newspapers constantly invoke 'principles' in politics but in most peculiar ways. Their tacit view is that in some, again quite mysterious, way politicians ought to have 'principles', but they cannot state nor describe what these might be. Above all, they have no idea how to relate them to the aspirations of the electorate and the winning of elections.

Hence, politicians are constantly portrayed as departing from (for very selfish reasons) some fuzzy, vacuous, unstated set of principles whose content you cannot discover except indirectly. You are told what a terrible thing political 'opportunism' is, and left to infer that but for its selfish display you'd have principle.

It will be observed that this is surely false: can't we read week by week extensive and clear-cut news about the content of such-and-such a principle in politics? We can, indeed. These mostly are statements which journalists or some of their sources have labelled principle because they come from a given context. That context is usually in some way formal, institutional, tends to yield written statements and may have a good deal of ritual. Bits from conference resolutions, party objectives, platforms or parliamentary statements are typical.

But who decides, and how, which of these fragments are the 'principles' and which actions are to be termed 'opportunist'? There are few journalistic doubts as to who is the noble soul observing principle and who is the unprincipled opportunist.

The hard news straitjacket cannot handle the most basic and difficult aspects of both ethics and politics. How often are we faced with a conflict of desirable principles? How can we trade off goods which clash? How frequently do we face a number of opportunities and have to choose between those? Moreover, what are we to say of context and the fact that for politicians this changes, again and again, due to factors beyond their control?

Journalists, also, just as they seem to assume that there can be a clear-cut consensus-based notion of 'politics' seem to believe the same of 'principle'. Yet in politics what is to be seen as principle and what as its breach are themselves decisions which are part of conflicting interests and ways of life. To wear the label of 'principle' on the one hand and that of 'opportunism' on the other is believed to be advantageous and harmful. Hence your actions are never opportunist but 'realist' or 'practical' while those of your opponent are not 'principled' but 'dogmatic', 'unrealistic', 'fanatic', 'hard left', 'hard right'.

What is a principle's relation to other norms? In what sense is it binding, on whom and in what contexts? How is it related to legitimacy or to winning elections? All these questions are part and parcel of the political struggle itself. Journalists report on 'principle' and 'opportunism' as if they were similar to statements about the weather.

Hard news may need this way of conceptualising—a clear-cut principle with a clear-cut breach makes for drama, simplicity and tension—the same illusions as apply to a clear notion of a narrow self.

Through this way of writing the political process is robbed of its many contexts and appears as both more vacuous and more deterministic than it can reasonably be said to be. There might be principles in politics which all agree are principles, whose status is uncontested and whose meaning seems clear. If they exist then they are either at a very high level of abstraction and have not yet been challenged or else they are taken-for-granted assumptions which must be looked at through some kind of sociological lens or lenses.

In politics, then, principles (and of course 'opportunities') are multivocal and multiperspectival.

Why is this inability within the hard news dimensions to treat 'principles' in politics reasonably so important? Because it means you cannot tie up principles with decision making and, in this context, with decision making modes thought of as 'democratic'.

It is a widely held view that one can distinguish political systems in terms of the relationship between popular choices, political issues and political outcomes. To what extent such links exist now, how in turn popular choices are fashioned, whether choices can be or are influenced by outcomes—these are all contested but the ideas of such linkages much less so. Elections can be seen as one regular mode in which such linkages are or are not disputed. Insofar as one wants to talk of principles in politics it becomes important to try and think of elections as related to principles. The way the press treats principles makes this very hard.

The point about the rigid reductionism in the press's concept of both 'the self' and of 'principle' also means that news treatment is especially skewed against anyone who wants to claim a new, different motivation for political action or who claims to have moral aims in issues which relate to a set of principles. This point applies to a wide range of interests—the Fred Niles or Santamarias, the Democrats, or the Communist Party of Australia. It works even more forcefully against those who reject the standard left/right dichotomy: libertarian free marketeers, radical feminists and the greens.

Issues

One could write a book on how 'issues' are conceived, shaped, nurtured and killed in the press.

Issues are seen by many journalists as inherently boring. The idea that news is self-generating has been knocked by so many people that it is now less widely accepted even among journalists. But the notion that if something is 'an issue' and if it cannot be 'personalised' then it must be boring (so that readers will stop and viewers switch off) is still very common.

Interest and boredom are no more 'natural' than concepts such as knowledge or entertainment. (Even *Dallas* was a flop in Japan.) As to complexity or simplification, there are inherent limits derived from the nature of the material. But even then it is usually possible to alter the perspective and look at the material from another angle. Surely it is part of the journalists' skills to make issues interesting.

It may be true that few people will yearn to see the links between the personal and the general. But, if one agrees that such issues as the budget, taxation policies, the assets test or the sudden 'discovery' that misery and starvation exist in remote parts of the globe, have to be 'related' to personal concerns, this does not get us very far.

It once more begs the question of how journalists ought to think of and write about the 'self'—here the 'personal'. This is never self-evident.

Nor does it follow that issues, once personalised, must appear as isolated fragments which rain down on increasingly irritated, puzzled and turned-off audiences.

You can start from the fact that all interpretations of society have notions of interaction, feedback and long-run processes built into them, though laissez-faire, conservative and neo-Marxist maps differ sharply once such notions are enlarged on and their interconnections analysed. As a start one can make some interlinkages.

Newspapers can be good at simplifying quite complex matters—for example, comparative benefits and costs of competing private medical health funds—and presenting such information in an easily accessible form. They are doing much better than would have been thought possible even a few years ago in supplements or long features on taxation, investment, crime and corruption, education and, more rarely, Aborigines. But these welcome developments go beyond the hard news format and are, in fact, magazine or magazine-like sections.

We know of no work on the two major questions: What kind of reader looks at this sort of material? How much of it is understood in what kind of ways by what sorts of readers?

Leaders

When the press accepts the party-generated focus on the creation, maintenance and promotion of the leader's image and focuses hard news on him (or, in a few countries, her), it tends to underwrite some very dubious assumptions:

- That democratic politics is determined by 'leaders' seen as strong or weak, bad or good communicators. Such a focus pushes aside structural questions. It also ignores normative dimensions. There is nothing desirable about 'strong' leaders: if they want to cut your throat or oppress you, you'd wish they were bad at it and were much weaker.
- Personality aspects and public behaviour as such do not enable you to make judgments about policy. You cannot link crying in public (even if not pre-arranged) with any policy issue and people who infer policy dimensions from lachrymose displays are childish. There are no linkages of a predictable kind between being or behaving like an 'actor' and having a policy you might wish to support or oppose. If you stumble when stepping from the plane it does not mean that you or, to be sure, your diplomats and staff will stumble in negotiations about nuclear armed ships or in deals with some set of domestic interests.

The press tacitly takes over and proceeds from trait concepts of leadership in which a given combination of personality traits constitutes leadership. The alternative way of thinking of leaders need not eliminate all traits but it puts major stress on context. A superb cricket captain need not be good at tennis let alone diplomacy or selling cars. A politician who is a good specialist minister may be a very poor prime minister.

It must be repeated that generally acceptable personality traits, even if they manifest themselves in a wide variety of contexts, cannot tell you anything about the normative dimensions of the policy—whether it should or should not be approved by you.

Background and soft news

The hard news formula has been much more rigid than that

part of the paper which is background, soft news, feature or, increasingly, combines some feature elements with a hard news aspect.

This element of the papers is increasing and it has vastly improved. No data exists as to how much of the news hole it occupies, what impacts it might have, how much of the 31 minutes a day spent on reading (perhaps better 'handling') the paper is devoted to it.

It is the most neglected part of the press: What criteria of journalism are appropriate for it? What is the relation between 'hard' news and 'other'? How far are the old and cosy distinctions of hard versus soft, news versus feature, meaningful in the 1990s?

9 The Press and the Public Service

This, the earliest of the writings selected, was based upon a talk to federal public servants at a time under the Whitlam government when bureaucratic politics and media coverage of the public service had for the first time become publicly problematic. Several characteristic themes are apparent: the inevitability of conflict, the variety of interests, the clashing standards and vantage points, the absence of evidence about key points. Despite the topic's obvious importance, this remains one of the few academic articles to address it.

These comments will have to be very tentative and speculative. That would also be true of any that disagree with them. No one has yet done the empirical work which might bridle the guesses.

We focus on the tensions between press (including television) and the public service. The argument is that such tensions are inherent in the way both enterprises are organised and see their job. The media cut across and to some extent undermine the conventional assumptions on which the public service rests. The press uses and must use criteria to judge costs and benefits of publicity and information which are not those usually used by the public service.

I

One of the standard clichés about the press is to claim that it lives by disclosures. That is misleading. The way it is usually put suggests some band of bold, autonomous, jousting press knights, free and unblinkered. The disclosures of the press are highly skewed. Of all the events and processes that might be put on the agenda, newspapers construct and use certain criteria for justifying selective disclosure.

News is not some kind of natural thing, like stones, found out there. It is socially produced and socially discovered. The element of creativity and shaping inherent in its production and presentation is inescapable. The same point can be made—as any one working on social indicators will know—about 'hard' statistics: what is recorded, what counts as a record, the way it is organised—all these are socially contentious.

The most important question to ask about the news in general is how and why it is skewed the way it is: how the skewing is transmitted in the occupational structure; what consequences for the social structure flow from it; what kinds of alternative skewing are present; at what costs are they available and to whom; and what is the distribution of benefits and burdens tied to a particular skewing.

One way of glancing at the press versus public service issue is to look at some of the criteria currently used in the production of news. We can then, in a general way, relate these to what public servants conventionally tend to assert they are doing.

Inevitably one makes a major assumption as to the general outline of public service activities: that they do in a very rough way correspond and/or are in Australia widely seen as corresponding to the hierarchical–bureaucratic map worked out by Max Weber.

Press activities will tend to cut across and clash with the hierarchical–bureaucratic assumptions and procedures of the public service. This is so not so much in terms of the intentions of journalists, though these would have to be looked at most carefully in any less sketchy account. It is better initially to stress habit and what is taken for granted and to say it is rather the consequences of journalistic work styles.

1. Good journalists, given a chance, will have their own network of sources. Their assumption will be that it pays to go 'behind' whatever official information is available. At times they can secure another official and more revealing (or concealing) statement from the very top, but normally they will have to work on middle levels of public servants in-the-know and with background, yet still approachable. Their relation to such

sources and vice versa will vary. Yet in general such sources include a fairly high proportion of:

(a) Public servants, commonly middle level, who in a loose sense have not been socialised into the system to the extent of having the same conception of duties to the public as their superiors. By giving information at all they will display an informal network of power within the department and undermine the limits of publicity as officially defined.

    It is not usually possible to find out where the leaks come from—not possible, that is, at a 'reasonable' cost, since this presupposes some system of supervision which, to have a chance of effectiveness, would have to be so tight as to annoy and upset most of the department.

    This is why, on the whole, those departments which give maximal freedom to their people to talk and talk informally are taking the most sensible option. It is true that because of the very nature of the partly adversary relationship between press and government and hence press and public service, good journalists will tend to dig further. But their time is limited and, by and large, if they smell a story, they dig most where they are fobbed off most strongly.

    In general, the unofficial information will tend to be 'more' in quantity and more 'critical' in content than the top people would think proper to release. As you go to the top of the hierarchy, the scope and nature of information seen as potentially damaging to the department and the minister and as 'disruptive' or 'dangerous' increases. What is at stake here is not usually an attempt by the unofficial whistle blowers to disrupt but, rather, a different evaluation as to what is disruptive. Since the top cannot often stop leaks, such an evaluation is seen as a constant threat to its authority structure.

(b) Overlapping with the group which has a generally different estimate from the official one of what should be revealed to the press, but distinguishable from it, are those public servants who deliberately try to use the press to fight out specific policy battles. They have been defeated on an issue, or their views have not been asked for, and they now shift the locus of access and attempt to fight the battle once more. Such people would, one might guess, leak much more irregularly, and might defend the right to keep mum on most issues. Group (a) tends to be dissatisfied with the general official procedures; group (b) may be quite happy with them except where they have resulted in the defeat of the particular policies espoused by them.

(c) There is a third type of 'unofficial' information from within the service which is clearly growing rather fast. It does not fit in well with either (a) or (b). It is the quasi-official leak from or near the very top itself. If this is done by the staff of a prominent politician it may not be so novel. But, especially with the slightly more open role of the service, it is also apparently growing from within the service: the leak which 'everyone' knows was done at the orders of someone very close to the top, yet was not done 'officially'.

The journalists' total network then will consist of:

(i) the official material, whether it can be identified or is for backgrounding only;
(ii) quasi-official from-the-top information;
(iii) unofficial information not tied to specific policy battles but resting on a view of what ought to be told, not officially shared by the department; and
(iv) unofficial information specifically tied to policy differences within and between departments.

There is a good deal of information given to the press or obtained by it which falls under categories (iii) or (iv). Together this information has a structure which differs from the official one. There is an alternative information function which is in itself structured but on lines and criteria very different from those of the official hierarchy. 'Difference' does not necessarily mean 'conflict' but in this particular case it tends to.

2. Once a journalist interested in investigation, and with a paper or channel of some weight and autonomy (all important qualifications), has some unofficial information which is either true or would be embarrassing if released as it stands, even if partly false, some kind of official comment is hard to avoid.

Here, television is making it much more difficult to maintain 'No comment'. On TV someone to comment on whatever has been allegedly dug up can normally be found. No comment, a refusal to appear, or a plea of prior engagements does not wash well: the tacit assumption is that if it's on TV, especially on ABC TV, then it must be so important that someone should drop everything to be there. It is also part of the image of 'authority' that, in principle, it has 'an answer'. True that for the viewer 'the answer' is very often a total evasion or, in the case of TV confrontations between politicians, a gruesome non-event. But the pressure to be 'there' is tremendous. Once there is some kind of spokesperson, however remote from the actual public servants in the department(s) concerned with the issue, 'the department' gets potentially involved and is brought into focus. There is now uncertainty as to the outcome. This is an anti-routine function.

3. The press cites anonymous spokespeople or politicians, and TV overwhelmingly has politicians on the screen. It is not yet able to grill public servants directly. If we had a really imaginative public service and an equally daring ABC we would have had a regular Ombudsperson of the Air session long ago in which public servants explained why they do what they do, can be challenged and, absolutely vital, report back.

As things stand, there is still the impact of the interview, more especially the TV interview, on the public service. Consider: the reporters can treat the politicians in a way many younger public servants would like to treat them but cannot. The reporters tend to be young, tend to be generalists who don't 'stick to the point', and their setting allows and indeed encourages them to be much more irreverent than most non-politicians the interviewees talk with regularly. 'Irreverence' is part of the digging, probing tradition. It varies tremendously.

Most persons in authority interviewed both fear reporters and are potentially angry with them for merely being in a position to question and probe. On television one cannot predict the extent or depth of the probe, who will be watching and how far they will follow up. The chances of things going wrong are much higher. Politicians who hardly ever lose their cool on TV and seem to say a good deal with firmness, friendliness and politeness can of course score.

Exposure by and through the media, especially TV, has a counter-cocoon function: in its official capacity the public service spends considerable time spinning a cocoon round the minister. Officially there can be no recognition of differences in ability and political skill; all ministers must have woven around them a cocoon of authority and superiority by virtue of their position.

The media may reinforce this image, but they are more likely to present an alternative myth since the context in which the politician must operate is so radically different.

When you are in authority you are supposed to be good at everything—the higher the authority, the more incredible the range of things you are supposed to be able to handle. People's actual range differs widely, but while in authority you can minimise the danger of showing 'weak spots'. However, given its unpredictability, TV makes this harder. If you can control that situation by, say, having a list of questions beforehand and agreeing to answer only those, all may be well. However, the key point about TV interviews, after all the necessary qualifications—prepared interviews, pre-selected questions, wishy-washy interviewers—is that the risks that something untoward might happen are higher and are felt to be higher.

The media, over time, produce and present an image of the politician to the public service itself which has two key features: it has an appearance (mostly only an appearance) of intimacy so that the bureaucrat who has never seen the minister face to face can feel that he really knows him; and the chances are very high that this image will be less favourable than that which is propagated by the government and within the department.

The image widely held in the community and media-derived must affect the image building in the department and have an indirect but important effect on morale. Within the service, attitudes and morale in this field will be derived from (a) official attempts (of varying success) to maximise credibility and impact, (b) the informal gossip and inside-information network which exists at various levels and overlaps and interacts with (c) a media-based information and attitude foundation.

II

Possibly even more difficult is work on the second major aspect of the argument—that of the role of the media (here more especially the press) in communicating information, or clues to information, between and within departments. Control (if you do it) or suppression (if done by someone else) of information is very widespread. On paper such an organisation as a university ought to be a mine of information as to what others are teaching and thinking which might be relevant to what you are after. The very opposite is all too usual.

For the public service, it is only possible here to pose some questions: How common and effective are kite-flying information leakages intended to see the reactions of other departments? Is it possible analytically to distinguish between kites intended to promote a project and kill a project? The cases where a department briefs select journalists so as to try and kill a source of rival advice are the best known. Treasury's attitude to the first Vernon report and its linkage with financial journalists is often cited. Similarly, it will be fascinating to know what sources journalists used more recently when writing about the pros and cons of ministerial advisers.

The most frequently mentioned allegations concern leaks directed against another department—the use of the press as a weapon in internecine warfare. This is a highly sensitive area. It seems widely assumed that if there were a good deal of such leaks and (a distinct issue) if these weapons were not just used but used effectively so that, in fact, Department X would, via the media, exercise strong influence or power over Department Y, such an outcome would be irrational overall and hence 'bad for the service as a whole'.

It seems an empirical question how far and in what ways a given department takes the interests of the service as a whole into account. Rationalisation and being caught up by one's own ideology are very widespread. It would be odd if any given department at any given time were not sincerely convinced that its interests coincide with that of the service.

III

It is essential to emphasise that while the outcomes of news reporting are, in the sense outlined, counter-bureaucratic, the production of news itself is not a random process. As soon as one ponders two basic facts of news production, it is clear that it could not be so. News input is uneven, irregular, and unpredictable. And there is a rigid deadline by which a predictable total space must be filled. These two points, by themselves, make it clear that there is plenty of scope for what might be called the analysis of the bureaucratisation of news flow, and for concepts taken from Weber and organisation theory. Much of the better recent work hinges round the notion that what the news 'is' will depend on how it is processed and 'organised'.

Consider aspects of newspaper practice, deriving from news work, which annoy many a public servant.

1. Reflect on sloppiness, inaccuracy (whether purely factual such as the spelling of a name or in a wider and more interpretative sense), failure to check out stories and so on.

What is partly at stake here are clashing conceptions of time and time-bound risks, conceptions which cannot be judged in terms of a common scale of right and wrong. It does not make much sense to judge possibilities of accuracy without relating them to the availability of resources. Most Australian papers are remarkably stingy with resources. And the nature of news makes key resources relevant to the possible achievement of accuracy—time—very scarce indeed. Most stories won't keep.

To reply that the story should not be published at all till after more checking is to take for granted the time perspective of the service, with all its cost-benefit variables and the weights given to them.

2. As a second instance consider the stress on 'rationality' as good and on 'emotion' as bad. Demands by the public and by the press are to be downgraded by a process of labelling them as 'emotional'. When one listens to public servants here, one gets the impression that they believe that things and processes are 'rational' or 'emotional' by virtue of some kind of inherent procedural structure. It is remarkable that this belief is still clung to. It may be excusable in a period of great stability with no serious challenges where it is easy to identify the rational with the real. But reflect upon the creation of a new department—Environment—and what it stands for. It illustrates strikingly the social and political determination of what is 'rational' procedure, and the changing factors to be taken into account.

There is no room here to link this point with the whole challenge, which came initially from some people in Women's Liberation, to the existing concept of what is political. The slogan 'the personal is political', whatever its merits, illustrates that the nature of what is a political issue is constantly redefined in history, bar periods of long stability. Max Weber, when trying to define the nature of the state, was very much aware that you cannot do this by some specification of what is always private or public. If you try, you simply reveal your ignorance. Putting it differently, we may be on the threshhold of having rationality redefined or else ranked lower than it has been for a long time in the west, or perhaps more realistically among middle and upper class elites in the west.

As for the immediate future public servants will have to put up with much more 'sloppiness' in the press. They are in a serious economic crisis. Journalists are being laid off or not replaced, yet expectations of what they are to cover are constantly expanding. Independent cross checking will diminish—but clearly this might lead to quite opposite practices.

Similarly 'emotionalism' will increase; it is one part of a long and complex change and crisis in the established picture of the service, of professionalism, of research and of relations with clients and the public.

3. Newspapers have always been linked with some stress on the individual and the dramatic. They go in for personalisation in a way which upsets and irritates the public servant. They publicise the case which went 'wrong'. There are two typical departmental responses. One is used by whoever replies in the Sydney press to complaints about delays in having the phone installed. These are very good answers. They combine a detailed and clear treatment of the individual case with some more general background factors. In combination such a letter makes the action of the department seem reasonable, using a still widely accepted concept of what is reasonable.

The second type of letter denies that there ever could be a sensible complaint against Department X and then goes on to point with pride to all the cases where things went right. This is really fatuous since newspapers are interested in Kadi justice, in the individual case, and are not much concerned with the concept of impartiality and processing for large numbers. Here, again, it is a case of clashing norms.

If the specific hunches are no good, this would, one hopes, still not stop people from paying somewhat more attention to the assumptions about relevant practices which underlie so much of the conflict between press and public service.

10 Australian Mass Media and Natural Disasters

The diversity of audiences to which the papers in this book were originally delivered is itself testimony to Henry's stature and his commitment to promoting dialogue. In this chapter, written in 1979, he seeks to educate senior officials of counter-disaster agencies about the media, and about the peculiarities of media behaviour and impacts during natural disasters and their aftermath. Accepting that conflicting orientations are inevitable and that the authorities have limited influence on media behaviour, it urges them to eschew both the emptiness of codes expressing mutual good intentions and the undesirability and ineffectiveness of command-post, coercive approaches.

Let us start with a strong disclaimer: we are in no sense an expert in this sub-field. Having made the disclaimer, let us turn it round: maybe non-expertise is an advantage in *this* area. For having looked at the most often cited works[1] we get these impressions:

- Most of the generalisations are not established. They rest on a few case studies (many of them sloppy), on personal experience and folk-wisdom. On some of the most talked about topics, such as media accuracy in disasters, or media–authority relations, no serious study seems to exist.
- The material has its focus on radio with a little on TV and a tiny bit on limited aspects of newspaper reporting. Yet radio in general is neglected these days and we have very few 'effects' studies. Hence people write about radio effects in disasters without any kind of measuring rod and by

inserting necessarily crude psychological speculations into the cracks to make up 'bulk'.

- The stress in research is largely on output, effects, or as we prefer to call it, on impact: Does a given media content/mode have impacts as to fear, anxiety, panic evacuations, likelihood of heeding warnings and so on? However, in order to talk about *guidelines*, we need to know what the media do in the gathering and selecting process. News about disasters must be studied as is news in general, though it has a few distinct features. All news is an artefact and a particular construct embodying select aspects of social reality.

Agency and media conflict

Media and authorities are in permanent and inevitable conflict which springs from their respective roles: for the State Emergency Services (SES) the disaster is the focus and its total mastery is the main job. Any media aspects are but a marginal means to this end. For the media, disasters are just a type of news, one of many; the SES are authorities which can be criticised just like any others. Media are dominated by deadlines and speed. TV sees disaster as a moving visual ideal. Disaster items must compete with many others in the paper.

It is not hard for disaster authorities to work out guidelines for media reporting of disasters which satisfy moral demands and have symbolic value for drafters and recipients. It is very hard to work out any which will change media behaviour. To have even a chance it is essential to work out how media structures work and what constraints they impose.

A common approach by disaster authorities is that adopted by Oost (1979), who outlines three roles for the media:

- the news and information role (that is, the normally accepted role of the media);
- the disaster control role (such as the transmission of information and instructions from the disaster control authority to the stricken community); and
- the disaster information input role (for example, the transmission of appropriate information to the disaster control

authority, thus contributing to the decision-making capability of such authority).

He goes on to comment in terms of the pre-impact, impact and post-impact phase. He gives the conventional goals for the media, all from the perspective of the authority. They are:

- Give objective and concrete information which is 'meaningful to those likely to be affected' so that they can make accurate judgments.
- Be 'responsible' and 'accurate' in their reporting so as to reduce anxiety and alarm.
- In the post-impact phase locational, service and family separation information is vital.
- Volunteers should be discouraged except by permission of the authorities. Convergence should be minimised.
- Sensationalism must be avoided. Reporting must rely on 'official sources rather than rumour'. All this would enhance community morale. And the key sentence: 'In all stages of the disaster, radio and television can most effectively function as the communication arm of State Emergency Services'.

If such an approach is put forward media people may not openly criticise it and may even pay lip service to it, but they will ignore it. If you wish to have some real influence on guidelines, the following must be recognised:

1. Media are permanent institutions subject to all the normal constraints which are relevant to them and constitute 'their world'. For them the disaster is a piece of news and to a large extent must conform to their normal criteria of what is and is not newsworthy. These criteria include drama, human interest, the exotic, proximity, 'importance' (in terms of assumed impact on readers or numbers killed or wounded).

The disaster, if 'large' lives up to the daily lifeblood of a section of the media. That section has words such as SHOCK, SPLIT, HORROR or BLAST as its daily fare. In many cases their stories are beat-ups, the exaggeration of some mild and non-dramatic events or aspects. This section of the media will not suddenly reform and become an objective, calm, accurate, detailed handout sheet just because a real disaster has happened.

2. Media live in a competitive world. Radio stations compete with each other, radio competes with TV and both compete with the press. Disasters are tailor-made for television: they are dramatic and they have features which slide, collapse, blow up, flood and so on, all moving and highly visual.

3. The attention which media devote to a disaster will not be determined by the criteria of the agency or authority but by those of the media with possibly some minor concessions. The time of the disaster; the costs of getting there; its visual (TV) and audial (radio) aspects; the presence of stringers or network arrangements; the sort and amount of property destroyed; the question of who and how many got killed and whether they have 'prominence' in terms of news values—all these will influence the coverage.

4. Once the news input and selection process is over, disaster news must again compete with all other news. There is a daily ruthless struggle for space: of the billions of occurrences in the world, only a very tiny percentage are made into newsworthy events. These events in due course reach the paper after a complex process which affects their shape. For a radio station a lot depends on how they get their general news, and how far they rip and read what newspapers they are linked to or controlled by. In most cases the space or the time will not expand. You get sudden flashes on radio but these are very brief. The disaster item will most likely be cut further to fit in with others and will also be simplified.

The criteria of newsworthiness inevitably conflict with the goals of the authority. If there is no single authority it will, even in major disasters, assert its territorial rights against others once the first few days are over. During those days the normal conventions of bureaucracies do not apply or apply less. But this does not last. There will be conflicts, disputes of an intra-authority kind. From the angle of the authorities these conflicts are not newsworthy; they should not be news. From the media's angle they are clash-drama-split, and so potential news.

The authority will wish to have clear and specific material over radio, TV and the press. But disasters are—as all analysts stress—inherently ambiguous and fuzzy as to their 'meanings'. What is clear and specific is not likely to be the most human, to have the 'warmest' meaning: the authority will stress the aspects of the disaster which facilitate a (relatively) smooth and efficient operation. Not so the media.

Moreover, the authority is a bureaucratic organisation (as are media) and hence it cannot tolerate the admission of confusion and uncertainty. The media also seek 'certainty' by using allegedly precise figures, names and locations when in fact they cannot be obtained, or obtained in time. Hence the media in a search for precision make more mistakes. In the best survey (Scanlon, Luukku and Morton 1978) these were frequent though minor. The search for 'hard' facts is central to journalism. It gives the illusion of objectivity: if you have the names and numbers dead right that is taken to signify you have the true 'meaning'; it protects you against criticism and against the admission of uncertainty (Tuchman 1978).

The journalists on the spot have tight deadlines. The general situation, especially at an early stage, is bound to be confused. Despite the best 'plans' of the authorities, the nature of the counter-disaster intervention enterprise is not an activity which can be planned very tightly as a whole (although some mechanical aspects including communication links can and should be). Given confusion and given that bureaucracies especially with military/policy ideas think that to admit confusion is to show weakness, the journalists will have three options:

- To pool their rumours and cross 'check' in haste with each other. They trust their own 'nose' as to which rumours are worth passing on. In the process, some details are cut, others added, and the rumour acquires sharper focus (Rosnow 1974; Scanlon 1977).
- To rely on official information. But to the authorities news aspects are subordinate. They favour them only insofar as they can, with low costs in personnel and time to facilitate the immediate job at hand. Hence what aspect they give out will be scanty.

  Since disaster authorities typically rate news as low unless it is information which helps them it is unlikely that their information/public relations people will have high status. This in turn means that the media will not give them high credibility and rate their releases low, reinforcing the Catch-22 situation.
- To seek out and encourage unofficial information. In a good

> and influential US study (Waxman 1973) of radio in disaster it was shown that the need for news expanded. It was not met from official sources. The broadcasters hence became less and less controllers and checkers (gatekeepers of incoming news) and broadcast even contradictory news from all kinds of sources under an 'open gates' policy. (Another study [Kueneman and Wright (1975)] suggested the filtering of information for broadcast on the disaster excluded some information the authorities would have liked passed on.)

The most important clash between the values of the authorities and those of the news media lies in the nature of disaster itself: it is easy to report in its major impact phase since it is rapid, sudden, devastating and has 'colour'. But the disaster thus reported is an event. It carries little context and it is reported in a flash. If there is a slowly incrementally changing disaster it is less likely to be defined as 'disaster' by the media, unless a sudden crisis intervenes when the slow disaster reaches a disaster peak.

The point is central: our news media—with the exception of features in newspapers, unusually long public affairs programs on TV and magazines—are not structured to report long, slower processes. This is especially true of radio, built on fragments and speed. But the post-impact, bit by bit, work of the authorities, the recovery phase, is a process. This the media cannot handle in news stories. The broadcasting media can handle it least—they are the most fragmentary of the media, least suited for pondering over and for reflection in content about their material. What will they report, if they do report, during the recovery phase? Events which stick out; particular failures or crises interrupting the slow process. Negative news rates much higher than positive news, but exceptional heroism will also have a chance of being newsworthy. No wonder the authorities are angry: their slow and steady work is not mentioned or mentioned only in passing or in features. Things are bound to go wrong and these are what is reported: the events, not the continuous processes.

To summarise the reasons why media are so irreverent towards authorities and tend to knock them: media, even where they don't blow up stories, are competitive; they have a set of news values which are event (hence 'accident') oriented; they go for negative rather than positive news; if things go right there is 'nothing' to report. They make mistakes under the pressure of speed and the search for certainty to justify their job. A section of them lives on and by the clichés by which they describe disasters. They see that authorities do not rate news highly nor supply it fast enough for deadlines. They fill the gap with cross-checked pooled rumours and from unofficial sources.

Media, as such, are anti-government authority and are hence anti-disaster authority. They side with 'the people' against 'the bureaucrats'. They are contacted by atypical members of the public. They resent the low status of the authority's information providers. They may be influenced by the tradition of egalitarianism to write as if in a disaster all were equals except the uptight hierarchical authority.

This last, even more speculative point suggests that Australia's disaster reporting may link with what some see as a central characteristic of Australian history and social life, and others as a major ideological con job fed to 'the masses'. We refer to the ideas of mateship, egalitarianism and populism. Natural diasasters are supposed to strike 'equally' at all. Supposedly, since they have no human cause they are outside the social system and hence outside the class and power structure. (One must doubt how much of this is true except for those natural disasters which allow no warning whatsoever, whose effects do not hinge on the structure and location of one's house nor are linked with differential means of escape.)

If the historical-cultural context encourages the media to report them in terms of little battlers, the heroism, wisdom and strength of the people, the ingenuity and self-sacrifice of the volunteers and rescuers, the glories of egalitarian mateship, then the reports will be pro 'victims' and pro 'people' and will appeal to and perhaps help arouse a yearning for equality (compare the 'therapeutic community' material after Cyclone Tracy, Milne 1977). Equally, given the tradition against cops, tall poppies, the military in peacetime and 'authority' there will be an anti-official latent colour to the disaster story—the authorities are not victims, not sufferers, they get paid, have status and do it professionally.

Psychological principles

Let us say a little on what is known about media (and media warning) impacts on people in disasters. The section will be very brief. There is a good deal of conventional and folk wisdom, but very little of it is even roughly tested. The generalisations which seem to be best supported are:

1. There are very few panics. In the overwhelming number of cases where stories about panics, looting and mass hysteria were looked at the initial reports were wildly exaggerated (Rosengren et al. 1975). There is no agreed figure as to what percentage might 'panic' and no agreed definition of the term. But those who do venture a guess put it at from 1 to 4 per cent. They usually point out that this could mean quite a large absolute number.

2. No studies of any serious kind exist as to how far media in disasters promote or soothe anxiety (all very porous concepts).

3. It is agreed that mass convergence is a serious problem. It seems assumed that media and more especially broadcasts play a vital part in this. Though this is a commonsense and not a scientifically tested view, it is much the better to err on the side of caution.

4. As to warnings and information broadcasts there seems consensus on three points:

- Be clear and explicit. Suggest specific responses.
- The response will be best if there is belief that it is a 'coping response' which can effectively eliminate the threat posed by the disaster (Christensen and Ruch 1978).
- A full study of how people confirm in their own minds that the warning of information is meaningful to them is very complex. It must include assessment of sources, content, mode of warning, confirming information and its social context.

For lay people the key point can be put more simply: there is no room for a crude stimulus-response approach. You must find out how people interpret and construct meanings. You cannot assume that what is self-evident to you is clear to the addressees. In the Sydney Telephone Directory you cannot find the SES easily even when calm—it is on page 27. There is no reference to it on the inside cover of the book. Later in the index under N for Natural Disasters, you are referred to page 27. But there is no cross reference from D for Disasters, where we looked and the first five people we picked also looked. There is no entry. This is a tiny example. But the lesson is clear: get your views and instructions tested in a standard feasibility study, best where anxiety and haste are simulated. We suggest that once they have done the job they get an advertising agency to look at it. All the material must be tested for reading difficulty. (There are various formulae, that by Flesch is best known.)

Conclusions

This paper is written from the angle of a rational and enlightened self-interest of the counter-disaster bodies: it is not pro-media per se but is so in the sense that these authorities cannot win without media. They need them hence must learn to live with them and understand them as part of a counter-disaster role.

Media are in no sense extensions of SESs: if SES wants to change them it must either compel them by law or persuade them by offering them incentives. There are three basic approaches to media:

1. Moral suasion which has no effects on media but may assuage those who send out such messages. The usual discussion of guidelines is well meant and does little harm. It cannot do much good in the sense of actually changing the behaviour of broadcasters in mass emergencies. Its main role is symbolic—people feel better after the exercise. Since they do not have to do much such an approach is least disturbing.

2. Legal compulsion. This won't work, and is politically not on the cards. Hence the command-post approach must be rejected: no one will listen to the commands and they cannot be enforced. News media are autonomous entities with their own concerns and interests and modes of proceeding. They will not respond well to command-post language. They will not be in any sense 'the arm' of the SES.

We are opposed to a command post approach. It is obsolescent. But if the authorities wish to pursue it then they should do it in the relatively most rational way. That would mean exploring changes in the Broadcasting and Television Act so that legal obligations are imposed and made a condition of the licence.

Disaster research is following the general shift from the purely physical, engineering and military approaches to those with more stress on social psychology, political science, social work and media communications approaches—looking at totalities. On the organisational side the shift is also clear: it is towards a looser, less top-down, command-post approach with more stress on the quasi-spontaneous recuperative powers of the 'therapeutic community'.

Such shifting perspectives will not be easy: the social scientists find the military and engineering orientation impossibly simplistic, rigid and hierarchical. They are trained never to just 'obey' but on the contrary to ask for whys and wherefores all the time; the best of them actually do this with a purpose. People with a military/police/engineering background are bound to find the social scientists vague, conceited, undisciplined, too optimistic about other people. The sort of thing we are doing here will strike them as full of uncertainty (it is), rather loosely structured (it is that), not easy to grasp (it is not) and of little practical value (they are quite wrong in the sense that something like this is needed and at the moment it is the best that can be got. It could, clearly, be much better).

3. How can disaster news supply to the broadcasting and print media be seriously upgraded in quantity and quality? How can it become more speedy? What costs in accuracy is one willing to put up with? How can the credibility of the disaster authorities be enhanced? (We don't mean PR or corporate image approaches.)

Even if the disaster authorities decide that they 'hate' or 'despise' the media, it is in their own best interests to take the initiative and upgrade their media awareness, media consciousness, media involvement. The media will not and cannot, as profit-making private bodies, shift towards the authorities. You cannot clobber them. We have shown that there is little point (except to make you feel better) in preaching at them. There remains only the trade-off, quid pro quo approach. The media can be offered incentives which make it more likely that they will stop doing some of the things disaster authority people dislike and do some of the things they wish them to do.

Not the media but the counter-disaster officials must take the key initiatives. First see what you can do now with minimal disturbance. A number of suggestions are in the paper, such as upgrading the PR information side and offering the media more news. It is very important to start in a cautious way: people must be assumed to be anxious and worried about innovation. We do not criticise this. We take it for granted. It is much too hard and resource consuming to launch a frontal attack. Start with the gentle touch. But then do not stick there but go on to the next step. If you need a label try 'progressive incrementalism'. If you can, go faster later.

With more disturbance but still within the existing framework start an exchange plus simulation program. Second broadcasters to the disaster authority and get them into action. Let authority personnel work on media and write stories under pressure on disaster or do broadcasts. The government has an exchange program in which this might be slotted in. Use gaming and simulation to taste.

To endorse the media upgrading and then try to do the job without a re-allocation of priorities and resources—of money, people, knowledge and status—is not merely a waste of time, it would rebound in your face and discredit the whole approach.

Let us conclude with a more radical idea that authorities can and must live with uncertainty and confusion, cannot stop them, and indeed must be able to see their positive function. If we admit that disasters by their very nature are chaotic, are ambiguous as to their many 'meanings' and are dramatic, and that disaster reporting given speed (which the media will not and cannot surrender) must carry some of these features with it, can one use these facts creatively and positively? (Do not freak out please.) How far have confusion and muddled positive functions linked to flexibility and adaptability under stress? What is the difference between 'confusion' and 'flexible adaptation'? What are the negative effects (dysfunctions) of trying to cut out 'confusion' and what is their effect on efficiency and costs?

New Media

11 The 'Information Revolution'

This previously unpublished address to senior executives in 1981 raises pertinent general themes about the 'information revolution' typically submerged in more specialist and particular considerations of change.

It is hard to associate Australia with any kind of revolution. We do not embrace even mild changes fast. There are dozens of complex public policy issues linked to the information revolution. All I will do here is, in the loosest terms, draw attention to four: the politics of definition; the changes in power; the issue of national sovereignty; and changes in property rights.

The politics of definition

The concept of the 'information society' is very broad. When the leading US expert, Dr Marc Porat, says that the US and Japan have over 50 per cent of the economy tied to 'information', he includes data processing, education, research and development, telecommunications and advertising. The standard attempt is to classify a primary information sector which produces, processes and transmits information and a non-information secondary sector which consumes it as part of its normal activity.

In practice, if you classify by occupation, you ignore product and stress the contribution to the process. If you classify by industry you ignore the occupation and process. On ploy I: a clerk in a glue factory, but not a cleaner there, is an 'information worker'. On ploy II: a school cleaner is an 'information worker' but not the clerk in the glue factory.

There is not, nor can there be, consensus on what is to count as 'information'. Philosophers have spent thousands of years on debate about 'the nature of knowledge' versus 'opinion'. Teachers of 'communication' have never been able to agree what it is. 'Information' can be conceptualised as a commodity, a resource, a public good, or a theoretical construct. Particular pieces under its umbrella must be and must remain highly controversial—think of the can of worms opened up by classification of advertising as information.

The operational meaning of these concepts will only be marginally affected by what academic analysts might wish to say about them. One can at once see the process of conflictual bargaining in which issues of status, power and prerogatives—managerial, union, governmental—will be contested. As usual there will be the most lucrative field for lawyers, for union secretaries, and for lobbyists, especially in demarcation and tariff disputes. In the case of 'information' this mess will be genuine in the sense that even the most detached academics would have difficulties.

Power

The promises of telecommunications' uses are endless. They are almost automatically tied to promises of low or no pollution, falling costs for hardware, transport and travel substitution and costs which are distance insensitive. A future in which we can sit in our room (provided we have a job—this is always taken for granted) and tele-work, tele-shop and tele-play. Tele-culture is yours, tele-medicine if you are sick. A button allows plebiscatory tele-democracy. The approach in Australia is of a crude technological determinism.

The new services overall may increase the gap between the information rich and the information poor. It needs some level of specific concern to figure as a part of a more segmented market. Where this is not the case they may simply transfer to the home mass activities now carried on elsewhere, for example, gambling.

In many cases the services have inbuilt hierarchical tendencies. Cable TV is available as a 'basic' service and then builds up into increasingly innovative and expensive layers (tiers) of service. There is thus fragmentation, first compared with over-the-air TV viewers, then within the tiers of pay services.

How the lesser importance of distance will affect relative power positions in Australia cannot be foreseen. One may speculate that it will increase the attraction of rural areas and cut down the relative disadvantage of a state such as Tasmania. But as soon as one thinks more carefully about this sort of point the complexities rush in and one realises how simplistic such a comment is.

Within the top elites there will be shifts, when managers and owners who are less hidebound, more risk taking, more able to see opportunities, will be in the vanguard. Since the US is the centre of greatest importance, firms that are US subsidiaries are likely to outpace purely locally owned ones.

Sovereignty

In the last two decades many countries in the Third World have opposed the idea of a free flow of information. They have argued that it is a one-way flow determined by criteria and promoting interests which are not theirs. They have also argued that alien cultural values threaten to overwhelm them.

The cultural dimensions in international affairs will be boosted by opposition to an industrial information complex. This takes many forms such as the claims to new types of allocation on international radio frequencies. The general point is always much the same and comes out most clearly on the issue of transborder data flows. Louis Joinet, Secretary of the Commission on Data Processing and Liberties, put it thus:

> Information is power and economic information is economic power. Information has an economic value, and the ability to store and process certain types of data may well give one country political and technological advantages over other countries. This in turn leads to a loss of national sovereignty through supranational data flow.

The transborder data issue is often discussed as if it were mainly a Third World vs Rich World one. Fears, similar to the Third World ones but in milder form, exist widely in Europe and most strikingly in Canada. They exist over the amount of US TV Canadians are watching and most strikingly over transborder data flows. The report entitled 'Telecommunications and Canada' (Canada 1979) concluded that the country's dependence upon foreign computing services would:

- Reduce Canadian control over disruptions in service resulting from technical breakdowns or work stoppages.
- Reduce Canadian power to ensure protection against other events, such as invasion of personal privacy and computer crime.
- Lead to greater dependence on foreign computing staff, which would result in turn in lower requirements for Canadian expertise and a smaller human and technological resource base upon which systems specifically geared to Canadian requirements could be developed.
- Jeopardise the exercise of Canadian jurisdiction over companies operating in Canada which store and process their data abroad.
- Undermine the telecommunications system in Canada by the use of foreign communications satellites and roof-top receiving antennas for the importation of data into Canada.
- Entail the risk of publication of information that is confidential in Canada.
- Give access to Videotex services based on foreign databanks emphasising foreign values, goods and services.
- Facilitate the attempts of the government of the US to make laws applicable outside US territory.

Countries which have been for a free flow position on US lines in the UNESCO debates on news flow start worrying about satellite 'invasion' as soon as they see it possibly affecting them. Their language is then, in milder form, that of the Third World: an appeal to national sovereignty, a fear of it being undermined. Satellites and cable may permit the undermining of local customs, laws and regulations. It is important to recall that, for most of Europe, broadcasting is state run and advertising, where it exists at all, is in blocks, minimal in frequency and confined to strict times. All this is threatened, given certain satellite usages. Over 60 nations have now some kind of control over aspects of data flows, at least on paper.

Property rights

The information revolution radically affects existing property rights in two major ways:

- It leads to a blurring of the old distinctions between types of media and modes of transmission. Electronic newspapers—which may eventually become available in hard copy—are a good example. That means that the definition of the matter as 'print', as 'broadcasting' or as something new makes major differences to possible controls and to the opportunities of new challengers.
- It makes copying much more valuable and leads to endless and highly profitable attempts at this—of books, articles, records and computer programs. As software costs become relatively more important than hardware, the incentive to copy is heightened. The attempt to work out new protections for owners and the whole issue of intellectual property will lead to major conflicts. Patents, trademarks, secrets and attempts to have gadgets which will 'stop' copying will be major issues.

Information does not have the same psychological stereotypes as other property. If you 'rip off' the artist, owner, or whatever it is someone whom you've never met and who is remote. Property rights, whatever the legal controls and the technology used to shore them up, will be very hard to protect in this field. And, of course, the people who made an original contribution to the information or knowledge or entertainment, the artists, will make both economic claims and new moral claims.

Finally, there will be a demand for access to, and the shaping of content of, databanks. How can the weak, the poor and the minorities get their perspectives into them? All the old problems of access, control, diversity of options and so on have not gone away. Rather they will become more important and affect even more people more critically than the current media do.

Our public figures and parties and pressure groups have not yet done much serious thinking on such issues. How much longer will they wait?

12 The Cable Decision: Underlying Issues

In the early 1980s the most fundamental proposal for far-reaching change in the media was for the introduction of cable TV or subscription TV via some other means of delivery. After a long hiatus, these issues re-emerged on to the policy agenda in the early 1990s. Characteristically, Henry threw his intellectual efforts into these issues, writing two major papers. The paper presented in this chapter, delivered originally to a major conference at the University of New South Wales, concentrates on the inquiry process itself, the way our policy-making processes handle major innovations in all their uncertainty and complexity. The following chapter, published originally in a prestigious international journal, seeks to uncover the social presumptions in the major strands of public commentary on what the future of cable TV might bring.

This chapter is based upon a study of all 188 submissions to the Australian Broadcasting Tribunal's cable and television services inquiry. It comments on features of the inquiry process and then looks at key issues which underly the bulk of the submissions for and against the rapid introduction of cable TV.

Most of the submissions are by firms, institutions or people with a clear self-interest to protect or advance. Maybe eight or nine, just over 5 per cent, cannot at once, and without lengthy dispute, be labelled that way. The self-interested ones may, of course, in part or in whole, happen to coincide with some wider and more general set of interests.

As an old broadcasting inquiry hand, who has waded through the bulk of submissions in most major inquiries in the last four years, the most obvious difference is the novelty of the subject which brought to the surface a host of new interests and which is the first inquiry where terms such as informatics and compunctation have crept in, a long time after they have already become stale abroad. The novelty is crucial and we come back to it later.

When we undertook to do this paper we had planned to read the submissions, sort them into major options, and comment on these. This very soon proved impossible. The reason is of importance to others: in 1981 we took an active part in an Australia Council working party. We learned a lot about cable, but as an advocate. The self-interest, that of the arts, was a 'nice' one, yet it provided an end towards which cable might be the means. At the time of this work we did not have to be concerned with whether there should or should not be cable. Advocacy clearly acts to focus and narrow issues you have to address. For an advocate the gaps, caused by the lack of hard evidence, will be filled by ideology and rhetoric and selective 'evidence'. For some a strong ideology 'answers' the questions before they are asked.

Any academic not tied to major social interests outside the academy must be realistic as to his or her possible contribution: it may be intellectual, in terms of a search for truth and analysis, but, if so, that will be almost entirely within the still very tiny, but growing, ring of people now interested in such issues. As to others they will pick out whatever bits will suit them and use these as they wish.

If one tries, as we do, to be constantly aware of the existence and press of clashing interests in our society, and yet attempts also a slow improvement in the rationality of the policy-making process, the public contribution to its formation, and discussion of its outcome, one has no option but to cast one's bread onto the waters. In looking at some of the longer run issues, we at least put them on the record.

Roles of the broadcasting tribunal

From July 1980, when a decision to introduce cable TV was announced, through to December 1980 when it was decided that the Australian Broadcasting Tribunal (ABT) should inquire not merely into the 'how' but into 'whether', to May 1981 when radiated subscription television (STV) was added to the terms of reference, there has been a good deal of local industry and overseas activity but little public concern. In a society more convinced of the importance of communications, there would by now have been a reasonable coverage in the electronic media—especially the ABC. This has not taken place. The print media coverage, given the absence of cable and cable experience in Australia, and the predominantly whizz-bang and dramatic approach currently in fashion in the US, is not too bad by widely accepted standards of 'reasonable' coverage. Those standards themselves need constant informed criticism.

The public hearings of the ABT make it appear a much less rational body than it actually is. They are the most visible part of the inquiry process. Given our legal system, they focus on advocacy. There may be links between a particular example of advocacy and a search for truth. If so, they are contingent. It is the system of advocacy as a whole combined with the ABT which is assumed to inject rationality into the process.

The ABT's de facto functions are a complex mixture of gatekeeping, research, antennae quivering to the currents of 'experience' and politics, offering a focus for the mobilisation of latent interests and quasi-judicial and administrative roles.

Symbolic politics is one of the ABT's major roles: that is, whatever tangible changes in the allocation of resources come from it, a major function of the ABT is to make the public feel that a rational and equitable process has taken place and to offer psychological hearings, some symbols of equity, a fair go for major interests, and publicity for a 'detached' process. It is stuck with contested symbols such as participation, property rights, responsiveness and accountability. Many critics, very naively, write as if the ABT had earned good or bad marks by performing well or badly in terms of such concepts. This is a common view amongst reformers and, when it suits them, among some lawyers. It assumes that there is some consensus about, or at least a clear legislative or legislative/administrative definition of, such concepts. It then becomes the task of the ABT to implement or 'administer' them.

Whatever views one can discern from the ABT's decisions or reports (Administrative Review Council 1981), such a perspective is misleading. It pretends that the 'muddle' and 'incoherence' one sees is, in large part, a matter of procedures.

Some of it, to be sure, is, and it is worth trying to clear this up. But the bulk of the difficulty cannot be fixed that way: there is often nothing clear for the ABT to implement. What it discovers more or less clearly, more or less efficiently, and more or less visibly, is that 'the public', 'accountability', 'responsiveness', 'social responsibility' and so on, however they are defined in legislation, are permanently contested terms. Most of their content is decided by the struggle of interests in society. The ABT itself is de facto a major interest in that struggle and in turn helps to shape it.

The ABT does not, in any crude sense, 'reflect' interests. American writers often claim that the regulatory agencies are 'captured' by the interests they should regulate. But this is to assume, which we deny, that there is some state of affairs in which they would be free from, and above, all social interests or all particular ones. It is also to assume that such bodies could themselves not be a special part of the interests they administer.

The history of administrative law and of bodies such as the ABT must look, and look seriously, at the attempts to isolate such bodies from the battle of interests and, indeed, to remove them from it altogether. It must look at how far the ABT is itself aware of what its sociological role is. It must examine the important part which legal fictions play in that role itself. They are not merely 'superstructure' or 'tokenistic'.

The key issues to look at are: the extent and kind of ties with what social interests; the absence of ties and what this means; and how it comes about and may change. This must be done with sympathy for the aims of the process, but with a minimum of illusions about it.

The public hearings are the least rational part of the process because in them the symbolic role of the ABT is most visible. Role playing by ABT members, and especially the Chairman as giving 'tone' to the body, of the lawyers and of public servants and even of the witnesses and audience, is at its most formal. The apparent absurdities of the process are clearest. Few are 'absurd'—they all help shape the precise relation of the ABT to sets of interests.

The public hearings most dramatically display two abstractly irreconcilable aims: one, to show off a body which is standing above the battle of interests; the other, to show off a body which has inputs from major interests and which has simplified the complex issues coming before it into a form which can be processed in a short time and which is seen as making decisions related to 'the real world'.

Insofar as the ABT does not wish to be overridden by the government of the day, and get into the ignominious position of the old Australian Broadcasting Control Board as to television licence recommendations, it must, of course, try and strengthen its formal powers and independence. But it must also, in ways which have never been studied, try and raise the political costs of the government overriding it in various ways. The key question is how high are the political costs of upsetting whatever legal 'independence' there seems to be.

These comments must suffice here. They are rather complacent since they do not touch on much more difficult and disturbing issues: how to get new and weak interests into the system and legitimate them; what to do about inequities in the structure of interests; how to raise the costs of a given ABT decision not being implemented; and how to tackle inefficiencies within the ABT's inquiry process which do not arise from its overall functions.

The inquiry process

In the very early stage interests are skewed. In a new field, in which experience and awareness are in themselves unusually differentiated, the skewing is even more visible. There is a wide range of interests, some minorities (feminists and anti-feminists, down—or is it up?—to the delightful 'Women Who Want to be Wombats') or free-market deregulators or Australian Democrats to mainstream segments (the National Country Party, small business, the Australian Journalists' Association) who did not make any submissions. One must assume that an unknown proportion would have done so had their awareness of relevance been different.

There is nothing in the inquiry process which gives the submitting and major interests an incentive to use their time and resources to give their views and present their ideologies on broader long range issues: the relation of cable to alienation, to information overload, to 'needs' not charted by market research. The privacy issues do get some mention in some submissions. The broader issues are either used as a matter of 'knocking' the opposition or are raised by outsiders.

It has often been argued that developments in this field will become increasingly complex, the effects on a wide range of interests less obvious yet more important. Hence the inputs from 'the informed general public', itself a tiny proportion of the 'general public', will shrink further especially given scanty resources and the many inquiries which compete for their attention.

We share these concerns but now consider them as but one phase of an argument which needs enlarging. Taken as self-contained, it is inadequate. Insofar as the points hold, they assign to the ABT's inquiry process a responsibility which must be that of a more embracing body, like a general Communications Information Centre (a usually unmentioned part of the ALP's platform).

In a case such as cable, where there were endless rumours as to who might be interested in what, submissions have many functions. They give an indication—clearly imperfect—as to who is serious about what and hence give some shape to the structure of interests. The procedures give structure to interests so that they can be handled as inputs by a public service body, and hence are a foundation for stability and getting the process started (Bruce Gyngell's 'getting the show on the road'). But structure is not a neutral term: it means exclusion or downgrading as well as order.

What the ABT can reasonably be expected to do must be looked at in the context of existing concerns. There is a 'good deal more' the ABT could do if it wished to be more 'activist'. But, if you look more carefully at this general statement, it breaks down at once into a very few fields where the ABT's potential action might have a chance. Let us assume it did 'more' about children's TV or even about the most controversial issue of advertising to children, not allowed in Canada for children under thirteen and non-existent in many European countries.

Here it would have a chance since there is an actual constituency for it: people with experience of, and ideas as to, 'TV and children; people with few ideas but vague guilt feelings; the set of Senate inquiries; the work, which has made a good deal of impact, of the ABT's Children's Program Committee; the existence of some Australian academic research; and so on. It is no accident that the only research funded by Australian commercial TV is in this field. A history of this 'constituency' would have to decide how far Bruce Gyngell helped to create, or 'merely' shape, it and what the role of the many interacting forces was.

It is not hard to think of ways by which public participation in the children's TV field might be increased; it is much harder to think of fruitful and intelligent ways in which this might matter. But all the old methods of pamphlets, green papers, seminars, conferences, inquiries and so on, however slowly they work, have something to get hold of. Moreover 'children' are in themselves a symbol which evokes care, nurture and protection and we have now the outline of an actually emerging institution, the Australian Children's Television Foundation, around which action, in support, criticism or both, can gather.

In a new and much more technical field such as cable and STV it is hard to see much sense in such activities at an early stage. One must have unwarranted confidence in the force of education per se or in the way issues, abstract and remote to most, with highly uncertain solutions can be made relevant to favour a long process of discussion. Such a demand does make sense provided other and major shifts of resources take place, and provided that major efforts were made to look at how new technological developments with social impacts can be popularised. No one has yet seriously looked at such issues: the stillborn Broadcasting Information Office might have. The assumption must be made that they are worth looking at—but not that a sudden out-of-the-blue debate on cable would not have been a waste of time.

People who, like ourselves, believe in giving reason a go, must try to counteract gaps and make up for social differentiation. But again, equity is not a costless value and won't work well under all conditions. So we put it on the backburner ('conservative') but also institutionalise the matter so that it can and must be re-examined, say, every five years ('progressive').

A valuable step in securing a more fruitful pre-hearing stage has been the setting up of a Technical Working Group, to elicit some agreement on hard data which could not be obtained from submissions. The interests and assumptions on specific points emerge more clearly, the alternatives which are not mainly rhetorical can be discerned and people can work in a much more flexible way. The argument put by conservatives against constant public displays—that they must lead to grandstanding and rigidity and are in any case always accompanied by behind-the-scenes deals which show some flexibility and bargaining—has to be taken seriously. No more so, however, than the standard 'progressive' counter argument. The given context determines the merits.

It is hard to see how any but experts could make a rational contribution to such a working group. However, the capacity of expertise to settle issues always needs scrutiny. The lay general arguments for and against, for instance, overground cabling are pretty obvious and simple: they boil down to an evaluation of the priority of aesthetic considerations over costs. More specifically, the argument is that cutting costs for private enterprise should not occur at the expense of an 'environmental pollution' shock to the public, including many members who won't even have cable. It is possible, in principle, to affect such an argument if you can show to a range of people who agree in general with it but are not intensely committed to it, that: (a) the service private enterprise will provide is very important to them or important to others whose values they endorse; (b) the visual pollution is 'much less' than they assumed; and (c) the costs of the alternatives are so high that the supposed benefits under (a) will not eventuate. However, that is somewhat hard to take very far since there is little trouble in pointing to general strong overseas trends toward underground.

The point, in any case, is that the bulk of these arguments, though presented in some cost/benefit terms, cannot be settled by technical considerations or so-called 'objective' data. Insofar as economists have tried to do this their models have become more and more elegant and complex but also increasingly remote from being usable to convince the many people whose visible pleasures will be affected. Even more clearly, whatever the value of cable and STV one cannot see how one could mount the sort of argument which has been used in Tasmania (the Franklin Dam) in terms of something ugly and unpleasant being an 'absolute' necessity. For cable it lacks even the most initial plausibility.

Such lay arguments can and should be made at the public hearings but leave aside a host of highly specialised questions for which the working groups seem right.

If the ABT 'opened up' the early pre-public hearing stage, this would not be costless. Someone will be dissatisfied. But that is not the point. The stress has been up to now overwhelmingly on the public hearings phase but the structure of other phases can and should be publicised to the small number of people interested.

Uncertainty and generality

In general terms, the present inquiry is an instance of how our society deals with innovations whose consequences will remain uncertain for a long while.

The major underlying assumption, which will not be challenged during the whole process, is that technological change tends to equal technological 'progress'. Given this view, there remain two basic tasks. First, the purpose of the inquiry is to establish costs and benefits and trade-offs within the overall progress assumption taken for granted. The other is taking market opportunities and market expansion as inherently desirable and beneficial unless evidence to the contrary can be produced, and to derive policies which will allow them to develop.

The 'benefits' are in turn largely conceptualised in terms of self-interests with largely rhetorical, public relations and ideological rituals claiming to link these with wider ones. For people deeply critical of our society and convinced that better alternatives are available, the whole process is unacceptable. Kathe Boehringer, one of the more sensitive and perceptive writers arguing from this perspective, declares:

> The drawbacks of this approach are obvious. Firstly, it reinforces interest politics, and the power of the interventionist state as agenda-setting and as aggregator of the 'national' interest. Secondly, it fails to query the identity and constitution of the 'you' who will be enjoying all the convenience. Thirdly, by asking the question in terms of what kind of cake do we want, and how

> much of it we would like, the issue of whether we should want cake at all never arises. The key question, surely, is: is technological change consonant with the social order we want? (Boehringer 1981, p. 105)

Most of the people present today would be puzzled by and impatient with her comments. For them the issue of what society we should want is not a problem: in the main they feel they have what they want and want what they have.

At a much more modest and less critical level, it is still clear that we have no agreed way of handling innovation and no clear repertoires of skills needed to do so. What we hope to show is that the way we approach cable TV, the manner in which the issues are defined and related to or separated from others, will make a major difference in the way policy discussion is likely to go.

Conceptualising cable

Cable has two major aspects, both important: call them the entertainment and the information aspects. The former refers in the main to programs, the latter to all the present and future services linked to wideband, computers and the information society. We will not make yet another list of these.

On major issues, there is a good deal of uncertainty in the US over fragmentation, advertising, relation of cable to other STV, and how far cable is already obsolete and will be replaced by DBS (Direct Broadcasting Satellites). Academics can simply opt out by saying that it is too early to tell. Businesspeople and the ABT must make very risky decisions.

If we take a broad information approach then:

- information, broadband, computer and communications issues will get higher priority;
- the boundaries between broadcasting, cablecasting and telecommunications will be stressed less and overlaps, commonalities and convergencies stressed more. The ABT itself will be put into quesiton. One can think of the possibilities of enlarging its 'communications', functions and/or creating a new body; and
- a host of major issues, each a nightmare, will be more than

> marginally relevant: employment and unemployment over a wide range, deskilling, alienation, isolation, privacy, surveillance.

If cable is seen as closely linked to the future information economy, then ownership decisions about it will enable licensees to assume a key position in a whole range of future developments. Links they may have with overseas firms and transnationals will appear much more important. Issues of sovereignty and transborder data flows will loom large.

Hence, irrespective of the motive and reasons of those favouring a broader approach with stress on the information economy, the policy consequences are likely to be in the direction of caution, of going slowly. Interests who want the cable right now will tend to: (a) opt for narrower, and more of an entertainment, focus; (b) downplay the links with many of the broader problems; and/or (c) downplay the complexity and uncertainty mentioned above.

Protecting interests

Most major submissions of a general kind want an ideal world: a guarantee by the state that their current interests will not be harmfully affected and the type of protection deemed necessary will be provided, and simultaneously, an opportunity to take part in the new bonanza now or later. Unions want protection for the jobs and skills of their members and for the jobs and skills of information-related workers. Commercial broadcasters have a very long list of laws which they feel might secure their economic viability. Within this framework regionals feel they need special protection from metropolitans and networks. Cinema interests want a guarantee of their viability. Realising that this is unlikely, they desire a hand in cable with priority in the queue for franchises. The ABC wants protections. Potential cablers feel a threat from Telecom and have some delightful material about the wickedness of established oligopolies and the need for new blood—theirs, of course. They want protection from the big ones, just as the big ones want protection from them. Telecom wants to keep its monopoly. Moral guardians, backed by existing broadcasters, want protection against porn. Actors want guarantees of Australian content.

If you do not understand how society works, you will be shocked. Is it not illogical and indefensible for, say, FACTS to press for years for self-regulation in its over-the-air bailiwick and spread anti-government regulation arguments yet pursue a policy that cable must be tightly regulated by governments?

But while it is irresistible to make this sort of point now and then in a public sparring, it is not a serious analytical one. Social policies and their advocates are not to be judged by the standards of a university examination. Moreover, in the sort of mixed and state-paternalistic economy we are in (in our view also, in more disguised ways, in more planned ones), you cannot take for granted that incoherencies, inconsistencies, and adhockery are errors which should be eliminated. In any given case, they may be at the core of the ways in which the system or a part of it actually works.

So far as claims for protection regarding cable are concerned: first, there is no way claims to harm can at present be assessed systematically. To do so would presuppose an economic study or survey of broadcasting and cablecasting. The key scattered data which are public are only a tiny part of the picture. Even if problems of confidentiality could be solved, a gigantic task in itself, you would then need regular econometric studies of the kind now widely accepted in the US by both FCC and the broadcasters. Over decades FCC studies were counterposed by industry ones, and over a longish period the 'harm' argument got weaker and weaker. Out of advocacy you can, over time, and given resources and strong administrative will, get some rationality. But no such process has started here yet.

The area of alleged harm and economic damage will remain the most contested for a very long while. This will create difficulties for the potential formation of coalitions: many people who overall are critical of commercial TV are also, on general theoretical grounds, inclined to think that in Australia there may be a good deal in the economic viability argument. They are not pro-business but are pro-Australian content and production. Hence, they close their eyes to 'wicked' profits and stress the need to maintain Australian quality and, of course, tacitly admit the very high costs of this and hence the need for the industry to make money. But, as long as they are faced with wild claims and feel that it is all a rip-off, they will not come to the party. Whether industry wants them, and in terms of what kinds of trade-offs, we cannot say.

But the coalition point must be stressed: over the very early stages of the satellite story we had a de facto semi-confidential coalition (not alliance) between FACTS, the regionals and some media unions. Over cable there are obvious possible coalitions: Telecom and its unions against private enterprise cablers; regional TV joined with urban academics who have suddenly discovered the charms of 'localism'; the Festival of Light and over-the-air broadcasters who think soft and hard porn might fragment their audiences and hence start loving purity; Equity and FACTS against a flooding of non-Australian content on cable which will make it cheaper and hence more competitive.

It will be a very long time till the merits of any specific claims to harm and demands for protection can be assessed in a fairly detached way. But the wide range of rival claims must militate, irrespective of their merit in most cases, against sudden and major changes. Thus they are likely to make an irrevocable decision now more unlikely.

Comparability

The Australian image of what cable is and can do derives almost entirely from the US. The bulk of the submissions—both pro and con—reflects this. The US-inspired message is very attractive to both pro- and anti-commercial people since it shows that it pays for commercial interests to do all the things their critics have told them they should but cannot do on over-the-air TV. It is amusing to read the main pro-cablers, Myers and Henry Jones, sounding like mildly left or small 'l' liberal idealists who love diversity, cherish minorities and frown on media monopolies.

The essence of cable and even more of pay TV is to forge the standard capitalist direct market links between viewers and suppliers. For historical reasons, and since there was then no simple way of getting people to pay for their broadcasting directly, this did not happen earlier. Once there is a direct monetary transaction, then only the amount people are willing to pay, the total revenue this generates, and legal restraints will limit what cable can provide. Hence both size and income are crucial.

The basis is, of course, the market. And the key point to stress is market size and the consequent major differences in revenues. We can take populations (240 million vs 14.5 million), but the best comparison is to take people in TV homes. Australia turns out to have but 6.75 per cent of the US people in TV homes, and conversely the US has 14.8 times as many as we have. Thus a program in the US attracting 1 per cent of people in TV homes is over 2 million; in Australia about 141,000. The capacity for narrowcasting in Australia is then likely to be much more limited.

Why should anyone but the shareholders be concerned if an entrepreneur made judgments about a cable market which went wrong? Above all, given the right to take business risks, in what sense has the public and the ABT a right to be concerned with them? We stick to the public: it has a legitimate interest since much of business takes risks if assisted by the government, hence taxpayers. Even more, calls on government and taxpayers cushion it against market failure. Secondly, the diversity argument is crucial if cable is to attract immediate public support. It claims not just that cablers will make lots of money but also that they will fill a major gap which commercial, over-the-air TV cannot fill and 'diversity' is centrally linked with democratic and pluralist rhetoric.

The conclusion must be that the figures do not preclude a given pro-cable decision but do preclude the uncritical general transfer of US data to Australia. There can be few direct projections without a careful local check. It is up to pro-cablers to try and show how other factors (special density in a business district, disposable incomes and intensity of preferences) might make up for numbers.

Once cable TV becomes clearly selective, then the whole range of equity arguments enter the scene. These are concerned with skimming, the neglect of low income, sparsely housed (rural) areas and so on. The ABC owes its origins partly to arguments of a similar kind—the inability of commercial radio at the time to make a profit in most rural markets.

The equity issues, either within a city, between large and

smaller cities, between mainland and Tasmania or between urban and rural, are even more difficult once you look at STV. The problems cannot even be listed here. However, it is touching to see tough-minded commercial firms and advocates suddenly convinced of the merits of taking 'equity' seriously. It is also revealing what dimensions of equity are thrown in the ring. None of the unions, for instance, consider that distinctions between strong and weak unions or between the organised and the unorganised may be just as much matters of 'equity' as those which they seek to stress.

Conclusion

The inquiry is characterised by an unusually high degree of uncertainty and complexity. Since the ABT and major interests must make decisions, the inquiry will see a constant search for the reduction of uncertainty. This is most likely to take the following major forms:

- By the ABT: a sharp increase in rationality and a much greater stress on the pre-public hearing part of the inquiry.
- By advocates and lawyers: an even more rigid than usual use of selective information combined with a desperate search for legal forms and instances outside the cable field.
- By the select public which takes an interest: a rapid escape into the most general and vacuous left/right rhetoric and ideology. However, the actual coalitions between usually conflicting interests are such that coalition building will run to some extent in a different direction.

13 Images of Cable: The Broad Social Impact of Cable TV

Five images about the long run social effects of cable television are outlined and analysed. The focus in all of them is on the diversity which cable TV promises. One of them denies such diversity: it sees cable as a clone of over-the-air TV. The second concentrates on but one new feature of cable—pornography. Three images start from the assumption that cable is bound to bring great changes with it. The first sees cable as equivalent to narrowcasting and posits an endless variety of programs which will, together, bring about a new and highly desirable pluralism. The second also stresses narrowcasting but sees it as leading to the dissolution of communities, the privatising of ghetto-bound individualists, the fragmentation of common experiences. Cable ends up as a means of producing narcissistic navel gazing. The third image does not refer to diversity via programs but rather pays attention to cable as an electronic nightmare—menacing privacy and increasing the surveillance by business and the state.

Some of the assumptions behind each image are discussed and it is concluded that cable is most likely to be a mixture of re-runs of the old over-the-air TV and some narrowcasting. It gives some chance for pluralism since it may be possible for businesspeople to make money out of it. But this will not be a natural or automatic process: a good cable system will have to be fought for by consumer groups and political parties and this will be far from simple or easy.

* * *

'Cable' has become shorthand for a long-running array of sentiments and arguments about technology and society; about regulation and deregulation; about the role of the state in protecting the viability of established private or public TV entities allegedly threatened by obsolescence; about the relative importance and value of 'entertainment'; about rationales for a governmental role in the whole enterprise; about the future impact of telecommunications, and so on.

This paper rests on a broad reading—industry magazines, upmarket newspapers, newsletters and academic papers—of material on cable TV in the US, Canada, Britain and Australia. A more truly cross-cultural study might well yield different images. No content analysis has been performed. Such an effort, given that the arguments are so speculative and diffuse, would be methodologically doubtful.

Cable TV is but one mode of delivering material directly to the viewer which he or she buys in various layers, packages or tiers from the provider. The two major aspects of 'cable' are quite different and need not be discussed together. One is its entertainment and news cablecasting function, the focus of this paper and at present the main aspect.

However, while some of the themes about cable today are much the same as they were in the first major US report by the Sloan Commission in 1971, increasing attention is being given to the links of cable with computers and telecommunications and to the add-on services, from shopping and banking to security and medicine. These non-entertainment services are at an early stage and are much less easy to grasp, much less visible (except for experimental ones such as QUBE) and much more heterogeneous in both mode and possible impact. Hence they have been mostly discussed in a general framework of 'the information age' or the 'information revolution' or as part of the telematics computerisation of society approach.

Policy about cable currently follows the trends towards deregulation. In the US regulation was to a considerable extent a by-product of the interests of over-the-air networks kept out of and threatened by cable. This has changed and all major networks will be deeply involved in and eventually own cable systems. In the UK it was a government hopeful of deregulation which set the framework for the Hunt report (1982). This stressed correctly, but in a one-sided way so as to apply the point mainly to deregulation rather than both to deregulation and to new and more flexible forms of regulation, that policy about cable TV 'is in many ways a leap in the dark precisely because it should be experimental, diverse, and attuned to local needs' (p. 5).

Hunt focused on the effects of cable TV on public broadcasters and did not attempt an assessment of all-over social impacts. In the Australian report only the short-run social effects were assessed.

Cable is in many ways linked to 'diversity' and the promise of leading us to an age in which highly pluralistic communications will be easily available and be in the interests of business. In this approach, it is not surprising that hardly anyone should ask what does and does not constitute 'diversity' in the media arena.

Cable TV evokes five broad and loose images. It will be best to apply a Procrustean squeeze and present the images in their crudest but also sharpest form.

Cable as clone

Two quite widespread positions will be sketched only briefly since we focus on those images which take it for granted that cable TV will have new (good or bad) effects on society.

If you believe that cable is a clone of over-the-air TV with much the same content, the whole enterprise must seem a confidence trick. However, once we ask why consumers would be willing to make a conscious decision to get on to the cable and deliberately pay their bills for the 'same' material, we can see that, if cable is indeed a clone and sufficient viewers pay for it deliberately and directly, this would seriously undermine all the criticism—conservative, elitist, or left—of mass TV content as in some sense a product of manipulation or hegemony.

Critics of current TV content should beware lest they be hoist on their own petard.

Cable as clone with porn

A variant of the first no-change position stresses cable's resemblance to over-the-air TV but then focuses, often as if it were the only thing on cable, on pornography—*Playboy* (which runs a cable enterprise) or hard core.

Clearly we have here an appraisal of novelty different from saying 'cable gives us lots of (new) sport, but so what'. In principle it could be linked with the theme of pornography as liberating, a means to sexual and personal freedom. It would be surprising if *Playboy* and similar interests had not produced such an argument, but we have not seen it. The opposite would be the standard arguments against permitting pornography. These have been largely linked to some types of religion (for example, Court 1980). More suggestive, and tied to a general argument about male-created and dominated language, reality-shaping, modes of behaviour and social structures, are recent works by feminists whose basic theme is that pornography is either directly, or via a given view of sex, 'about' male power over and hatred and domination of women. In the extreme case, it is about symbolically and literally cutting women to pieces. It is seen as profoundly anti-erotic.

Frances Bonner (1982), in a very perceptive paper, has argued that the shift to private viewing on cable or on video cassettes is a step backward for women: whatever few restraints against exploitation exist and can be taken advantage of in the public sphere, where people have to show publicly they are into porn, are now eliminated.

Whatever the value of the central and serious argument as such, for our purposes its challenge is its implicit denial of the value of talking about 'diversity' in the abstract. The friends of diversity via cable tacitly take it for granted that the new material will be, if not 'of quality', then at least 'harmless'. This need not be so.

Cable as kaleidoscope

Arguments and images about cable which assume that it will have long-run and overall effects on society can be analysed under three headings. Two—cable as kaleidoscope, cable as narcissistic navel gazing—focus on diversity. The third—cable as electronic nightmare—highlights privacy issues.

In cable as kaleidoscope, variety and diversity are equated and their multiplication is tacitly assumed to strengthen a desirable society. Cable stands for pluralism and, through community channels, for participatory and active democracy. It is minority friendly, access related.

The main stress is on cable's distinct function of narrowcasting. It is to liberate us from mass communication as seen on over-the-air commercial TV and put an end to mediocrity, the lowest common denominator, pappy blandness.

People who embrace this image can be predicted to discover and posit a long list of 'needs' not met by the existing broadcasting system. These may be actual 'needs' as 'demonstrated' by some unmet open minority demand, or potential 'needs' which cable itself, once it existed for a while, might help nurse into full existence.

To make much of this image, five sub-themes are essential. They can be pushed in many permutations:

1. You must maximise the number of channels so as to minimise problems of scarcity, allocation and priority. For the kaleidoscope view it is best to be vague and to talk of 'dozens' or 'hundreds' of channels. If you run short, you can always look wise and talk of fibre optics and 'thousands' of channels.

2. You must ignore and minimise costs, providing endless potential free lunches. Since commercial TV and radio also have promoted themselves for decades as 'free' so that they still can contrast their 'free TV' vs (pay) cable's evil 'fee TV', this is hardly a new gambit. It helps even more if you can slip in a reference to two-way or interactive cable without any reference to costs and no mention that few systems are as yet interactive.

3. Endless tiers and people wishing to take them exist aplenty in this vision as does a wide range of programs which are 'alternative' to commercial over-the-air TV and, perhaps, even to what exists on public broadcasting systems.

4. In the earlier days of cable euphoria there were many hints and statements that the big thing was direct payment, the consumer in the market place, with no or little intrusive advertising. These days have gone and people are rather more realistic about costs and about how much viewers are willing to pay. Still in this image advertising is played down or assumed to be bountiful and non-intrusive (maybe in block ads as in much of Europe).

5. Viewers' knowledge of the widest a la carte menu is

either assumed or flows from the kaleidoscope view as a policy demand. For community access and educational cable channels, studios, equipment, technical assistance and effective publicity are assumed as given or as easily provided. Again there is no mention of costs or who is to bear them.

No clear general image of society as a whole underlies this vision. Broadly it is Aristotelian (uniformity through multiplicity) rather than Platonic. It tacitly assumes not merely that a wide variety of interests will have a view or style they wish and can put forward on the cable but also that they will not, as in the next image, be oyster-like but, on the contrary, be like flowers open to a variety of pollinations. It is not clear whether such cross-fertilisation is supposed to alter people's views and attitudes but the general assumption seems to be of a tolerant lot of viewers who at least will pay attention to what others have to say.

It is best for this perspective not to specify the content of 'diversity'. Otherwise it would find unexpected difficulties. Or you can claim that cable TV's programs are not '48 times the usual rubbish' at all. The rubbish it offers is quite unusual. It is unparallelled, exceptional, astonishing rubbish.

Cable as narcissistic navel gazer

This image can leave many of the tacit assumptions and lineaments of the kaleidoscopic one intact, though it need not. It can go along with a view of cable as narrowcasting and, if not free, almost costless. Where it differs radically is in its view of the role of mass communication via over-the-air TV and in its assumptions as to how societies are held together, hence in its pictures as to what an ever-widening variety and diversity would do to society.

It sees current mass communication via TV as a major provider of common models for society and as the main way in which some kind of public dialogue now happens. It stresses that in prime time there are only a few major programs which divide the bulk of viewers between them. It emphasises the way in which children, adolescents and adults use themes from a common TV experience to link and talk about them. It sees TV, and more especially commercial TV, as the great common socialiser, the glue which binds society together. TV is the most uniform, most widespread and most common experience.

Cable and narrowcasting are seen as undermining common experience, fragmenting not merely mass viewers for advertisers and, hence, profits for networks but also fracturing what previously tied people together. Cable is felt to be the great privatiser, the medium for the oyster-like narcissistic inward navel gaze. There is a tremendous variety of voices but, on this view, a threatening, divisive and consensus-undermining variety which weakens the bonds of society and allows no public or common voice to emerge.

The very common equity arguments about cable—that it will only be available in the commercially most viable areas; that it will lead to further divisions and inequities between cable rich urban main centres and cable poor smaller towns and country areas; that it will be 'elitist' through its tiering system so that the more money you have the juicier and more multi-layered and exclusive your cable sandwich will be—can all be related to the narcissistic navel gazing image. This stresses, in many ways of which inequity is one, division, separation, isolation, non-communicating ghettos.

The equity argument can also be related to the oligopoly part of the electronic nightmare map to which we now turn.

Cable as electronic nightmare

This image has two sub-frames. Each can be stressed on its own, but it works best when they are both brought into play.

One is the ownership concentration theme in which private enterprise is seen as increasingly oligopolistic and as dominating the supply and, through tie-ups with film companies and ownership of sports teams, the very creation of cable programs and the control of cable systems. As cable has spread from its original rural basis in the US, it has become more and more capital intensive. Clearly, the days of a mum and dad system are over.

It can be taken for granted, in this picture, that large-scale private enterprise will not be friendly towards a decentralised pluralistic cable notion with genuine alternative programs: it will tolerate just as much diversity as it has to in order to optimise profits. Moreover, it is tied not just to other mass media, many of which compete with cable, but also to other major power centres in society. Hence, what might threaten its interests on cable or, better, what it fears might threaten its interests, comprises a very wide range of potential social criticism. It can include, on some views, entertainment which is pro-feminist or has role models of attractive anti-polluters or members of a peace movement. Would cable TV in Germany, once it exists, tolerate and roster 'the greens' if by then they have not diluted their views?

Interactive cable and pay cable allow, if they do not demand, the regular computerised checking of viewing and other social in-the-home habits of subscribers and, in spite of promises of no abuse of privacy, cable can be used for surveillance and for checking up on people. Given the links between large companies and other centres of power, there is a real danger of cable turning into an electronic 'big brother' nightmare run by a few large companies. From this angle what appears to others as sensible (for example, the entry of American Express into cable) merely gives more data on its customers to the powerful.

This theme can also be developed for the international scene. It can include the role of the transnationals and controls over the educational aspects of cable.

The equity argument can be linked with it: cable, far from letting the weak and poorly organised bloom, in many ways widens the gap between the information rich and the information poor. Insofar as information is power, so the information rich will tend to line up with the main dominant interests in society. It is not important here whether these be analysed in terms of class, elite, establishment, or status differentiation. It is clear that many variations of this basic theme, bringing in concepts such as hegemony or co-optation, are possible.

Comments

What of the images? A more comprehensive analysis would have to explore two theoretical points. First, to what extent do the cable images resemble images of quite different social processes? In what sense are they 'about' cable at all? For instance, the diversity as kaleidoscope vs diversity as dissolving social glue theme has some parallels in arguments about multiculturalism. But in that case it is not isolation that is feared but rather a blowing up, an ethnic civil war. Clearly, in the cable case, there is at present a much stronger imputed assumption that the new ideas, programs, types of news and so on will not mobilise basically conflictual interests. In the early days of video many people saw it as a tool of radical social change. Blacks, women, gays and so on are trying in the US to get on to cable, yet this is felt to be just a slice of the action and we have not seen any literature in the last few years which ties up cable with major radical change.

Second, clearly all these images have extremely partial and simple versions of complex sociological theories built into them—symbolic interactionism, ethnomethodology, theories of 'values' as 'glue' and so on. They also all lack any conception of how strata, classes or the state might fit into all this. The presence and absence of such traces of theory might be analysed in terms of concerns with the sociology of knowledge, the derivation of ideology or the social construction of 'common sense'.

Back to our much narrower theme: the most impressive, if put in a much more qualified form, is that of the oligopolistic electronic nightmare. It won't do if it is merely anti-big business, nor if it sees menace lurking only behind public enterprise broadcasters or telecommunication providers. Bigness as such, whether private or governmental, brings power with it. The one certain thing about power is that you cannot rely on the goodwill of those who possess it, though that goodwill may exist at times. While governments are formally more accountable than is business and are subject to elections, the difficulties which ordinary people have in making much of this difference are well known. The general mechanisms of accountability and responsiveness in our type of society are very badly flawed. It is true that things are even worse in other societies, including those which claim to be post-capitalist. But this offers little consolation.

Cable will mean the admission of some new private entrepreneurs to the ring of existing media oligopolists. But we can be pretty certain that it won't become a small businesspeople's enterprise. Subscription television, much less capital intensive and costly, may have more room for them. One can predict that over-the-air TV and newspaper empires will be tied to cable—the degree to which this will be permitted, and how easily they can get around possible legal constraints, will vary from country to country.

Media oligopoly is a crucial issue in democratic theory but not in the day-to-day politics of any western nation. The adverse relationship between media concentration (Australia has the worst in the world and also seems the country most indifferent to it) and democratic theory is widely recognised and runs across the left–right spectrum. But, given the fears of government intervention being worse than business domination, few countries have serious plans for divestiture.

If one is interested in action, then one must keep the theoretical point alive but concentrate on what are in fact mildly reformist measures though they may seem 'wild' and focus on the second strand of the argument—protection against possible invasion of privacy. Here lawyers can and ought to play a major part. And not only the state but also business and the unions can, of course, be privacy invaders via cable as, to be sure, the media themselves are most likely to be.

To confine our comments to the state: the modern state is, increasingly, both openly and clandestinely, a surveillance state. Cable will offer additional opportunities for surveillance and for business, or corporatist state-business, invasions of privacy. But this is not a specific point against cable: it is but one mode of communication in a computer-telecommunications age that offers such possibilities and it is hard to see why it should be singled out. Broadcasting regulatory authorities can, much more easily than in the case of oligopoly, do a good deal to control privacy/surveillance dangers in cable TV. But we repeat that it would be an illusion to believe that successful control of cable would mean a significant lowering of all-round overall opportunities for surveillance and for invasions of privacy.

The kaleidoscope and narcissistic views of cable both ignore careful calculations of costs and benefits and pay little attention to resources, and are thus poor bets. On the matter of resources all one need mention here is that each of the three US networks in 1981 originated 200 hours of original prime-time programming a year with average costs to them of over $US500,000 an hour. With about 400 network hours a week, 21,480 hours of 'product' are needed every year. Even when re-runs are taken into account, a lot of hours are left. How will cable compete for ideas, creativity, writers? Cable will have huge problems with US programs, let alone indigenous content.

Both images badly overstress the novelty of cable, seen as nothing but narrowcasting. Given the economics of cabling, the current interest rates and the cost of programs, this will not be the case in the US, let alone in countries such as Australia with 6 per cent of the size of the US market. Narrowcasting will happen. In some fields it may be the mainstay—business and finance, medicine. But, of course, that will mean relatively expensive pay cable tiers. It is not possible yet to say how much profitable narrowcasting at what prices cable systems in different countries will have. There is also, in due course, bound to be a legal dispute (if there is a regulation) as to how narrow 'narrowcasting' has to be.

Audiences for broadcast TV as such do not have to be wooed: they offer themselves, so to speak. By now there is no point in marketing TV as such to viewers. It is, to be sure, marketed to advertisers in competition with other media. Particular TV structures (public vs private), specific networks, channels or programs are promoted and marketed to viewers. But not television per se.

Cable, for a long time yet, needs much more marketing. It is, as yet, much less habitual. The same applies to a good deal of kaleidoscopic content, whether we think (as this writer does) that the bulk of it will be cultural rubbish but an unknown but worthwhile proportion will not be, or take some other view. A good marketing strategy can increase demand for specific (including 'worthy') cable TV programs and programmers. Cable, much more easily than broadcast TV, can make money for its promoters and yield some additional desirable pluralism. But those who want quality will have to promote it and the demand for it. Cable gives them a chance to do so.

We guess at a mixture of narrowcasting with much more mass appeal films and sport. A picture of cable TV which looks for its differences from over-the-air TV also in type and frequency of advertising and yet sees it as having commonalities as well as product differentials seems much less dramatic but more likely to happen. VCRs, time shifting, teletext, video games and Videotex will further complicate the picture.

Many of the arguments are fine for people such as the writer who enjoy irony: it is good to see tough, profit-oriented, over-the-air broadcasters suddenly worried about the social injustices such as regressive fees caused by cable TV. After decades of complaints about the rubbish that mass entertainment TV produces, about the terrible sexism of its role models and about its possible brutalising effects on heavy viewers who are also said to be full of fears light viewers do not have, it is amazing to hear praise for mass entertainment as the presumedly beneficial glue which holds society together.

Conclusion

Cable TV will give us some more variety and some more diversity of content than we have now. How much of this there will be, and just how different it will be, it is too early to say, nor do we yet know how much we will have to pay for a basic system, let alone additional goodies. Only those who believe in miracles will doubt that there will be much appalling rubbish. But there seems a fair chance of getting an unknown but not negligible percentage of the 'right stuff'.

What of equity? It is obvious that many country people will be at the end of the cable queue, if they can join it at all. But this is usually true of new technologies relying on dense population. Regulators can prevent 'cherry picking' in franchising. It is true that the poorer you are the less likely you are to be able to afford a basic subscription, let alone tiers. How one feels about this might be influenced, for instance, by one's views as to differential discretionary spending on smoking, drinking and gambling.

One should look at the possibilities of subsidised or free cable for the poor, the pensioners, and the unemployed and explore positive discrimination policies where cable content can be linked with the acquisition of more skills, more clout and more relevant knowledge by the weak, the unorganised and the poor. There is no question that cable will bring with it new forms of injustice. The proper policy is to press for government and private action to overcome these or minimise them and compensate for them.

Another equity aspect is whether cable TV will widen the gap between the information rich and information poor. Those with some money and skills and living in not-so-poor suburbs have, it is argued, a better chance of getting cable, being able to afford to be connected, buy tiers-a-plenty and receive information which will help them to differentiate themselves yet further from those who do not share these initial advantages.

It is too early to assess this view: it is an empirical matter what the cost of being wired up and of tiers will be, and what sort of discretionary incomes will be available from whom. We do not yet know what social conditions the regulators will attach to franchises and how they will monitor these. If they wish they could try and secure that deprived groups have a chance of getting into cable land. They can narrow the information rich/poor gap but, let us be quite clear, certainly not by sole reliance on market forces. This would require a policy of rate setting, rate control, rewards for differential rates in favour of the information poor and so on.

'Cable' as such is not the issue. Policies in specifics associated with it are. They are clearly political issues. Parties will have to be pressured if one cares for equity. Parties do not favour an optimising of 'information' or its 'just' distribution as such: they want less information (and power) for those who oppose them and more (of both) for actual and potential supporters.

So there will be no cornucopia nor a giant kaleidoscope nor an end to common and public intercommunication but a more varied menu, at a cost.

Since there is a direct market relationship and since cablecasting, unlike magazines or newspapers, is government regulated or, if Lord Hunt's views prevail, will have at least broad and general oversight guidelines, it is likely that, for the first time, some media consumers—the small proportion who are organised—will enter the picture.

This offers a major opportunity for the consumers' movement. It has a clear and narrow interest in issues such as rate setting and services offered by cable entrepreneurs, private or public. It has also a less obvious but, in the long run, more important interest in looking calmly and critically at the whole structure and regulation of cable.

In doing this, it should work out why in recent years there has been such a widespread reaction against regulation and see how far the complaints of the regulated are justified, and how far it ought to go in for more general issues of social justice. It is crucial that those interests, in fostering whatever pluralism cable can put up with or promote, do not have rigid a priori views as to what is possible for businesspeople.

They need have no admiration for our social system nor rave on about the joys of the market to realise that cable may permit the more rational businesspeople to be slightly more pro-pluralist than they were before and to make money from this.

There is little that is inspiring or noble in such an approach and there is no question that it will be seen by many reformers as a sell out, by many businesspeople as too idealistic. Yet, hopefully, not by all on both sides.

Endnotes

Introduction

1. This quote, and others similaly cited, come from a special issue of *Politics* (vol. 20, no. 3, November 1985), edited by Joan Rydon and Murray Goot to mark Henry's retirement. Donald Horne's comments were made at an occasion we held following Henry's death. Other speeches and a collection of tributes were then published in *Media Information Australia*, no. 61, August 1991. Henry had decreed that no memorial services be held for him, and this inhibited us for a week or two. But instead we decided to hold a celebration of his life and work. Whether or not he would have approved the occasion, he would have applauded the conceptual finesse by which we justified it.
2. Henry's reviews appeared in *24 Hours*, January 1980, and *National Times*, 27 February 1983. Quotes about the *Dunera* experience are taken from these reviews.

Chapter 1

1. Until its takeover by Murdoch in the summer of 1986–87, the Herald and Weekly Times was the largest newspaper group in Australia, accounting for just over 50 per cent of daily metropolitan circulation, and having substantial holdings in television, radio, magazines, theatre and records. It owned newspapers in all the state capitals except Sydney. Its strength also came from its comfortable monopoly position in the smaller states, many of its papers thus avoiding either the colour of the tabloids or the pretensions of the qualities.

Chapter 3

1. For decades the *Sydney Morning Herald* was nicknamed 'Granny' and the ABC 'Aunty'. It is equally interesting to ponder why both usages have all but disappeared over the last decade or so.
2. In 1983, following the Dix Report, the new ABC Act renamed the Australian Broadcasting Commission, the Australian Broadcasting Corporation. Consequently, the government-appointed Commission was replaced by a board with essentially similar functions.

Chapter 4

1. During the late 1970s, TV licences were subjected to public renewal hearings by the Australian Broadcasting Tribunal. The rules governing public participation and the admissibility and relevance of various types of criticisms of stations' performance were subject to considerable uncertainty. Under the colourful chairmanship of former commercial TV executive Bruce Gyngell, they were marked by dramatic episodes. None was more dramatic than a sharp public clash culminating in the resignation of fellow Tribunal member Janet Strickland, who was seen as more sympathetic to the public critics.

Chapter 7

1. At this time, the advertising of tobacco products on radio and TV was still legal, although there was strong pressure, ultimately successful, to have it banned.

Chapter 10

1. As with all chapters, much of the discussion of then current references has been eliminated. However, the following observations are notable: 'One longs for cross-cultural work which should include countries claiming to be non-capitalist and Third World countries. Research whose basic assumption and methods are so closely tied to only one culture tends to be criticised from too narrow a range of views. It tends to take its own culture for granted.' Two pieces of work are particularly praised—a Swedish study which 'combines standard US survey techniques with in-depth and a more speculative sociological-

anthropological approach. These allow a much more stimulating analysis of the *symbolic* aspects of diasters' (Rosengren et al. 1975). The other is the Canadian, Joseph Scanlon, whose study 'Day One in Darwin' is praised, as is his whole approach: 'Professor Scanlon (1979) is in the very rare position of being able to send out his team just after a crisis and then being able to compare what he calls "what actually happened" with media accounts and to note the differences' (Scanlon, Luukku and Morton 1978).

References

A. Original sources of chapters by Henry Mayer in this book

Chapter 1 'Media: images and arguments', in *Australian Politics: A Fifth Reader*, eds Henry Mayer and Helen Nelson, Longman Cheshire, Melbourne, 1980.

Chapter 2 'Media: control, accountability, influence', previously unpublished paper given to forum at Murdoch University, 1982.

Chapter 3 'Media diversity reconsidered', in *Communications in Australia*, ed. Ted J. Smith, Warrnambool Institute Press and Australian Communication Association, 1983.

Chapter 4 'Dilemmas of mass media policies', Seventh Annual Lecture, The Academy of the Social Sciences in Australia, Canberra, 1979.

Chapter 5 'Right of reply', previously unpublished submission to Australian Broadcasting Tribunal Inquiry, 1989.

Chapter 6 'Censorship: trends and paradoxes' in *Entertainment and Society*, ed. Geoffrey Caldwell, AGPS, Canberra, 1977; also in *Quadrant*, 1978.

Chapter 7 'The morality of political advertising', *Journal of Australian Marketing, Advertising, Communication*, no. 1, 1980.

Chapter 8 'Images of politics in the press', *Australian Journalism Review*, 1985. Reprinted in *Issues in Australian Journalism*, ed. John Henningham, Longman Cheshire, Melbourne, 1990.

Chapter 9 'The press and the public service', *Newsletter of the Royal Institute of Public Administration* (ACT group), July 1975.

Chapter 10 'Australian mass media and natural disasters', *Report of Proceedings of the Media Study Group, Natural Disasters Organisation*, Department of Defence, Canberra, 1979.

Chapter 11 'The "Information Revolution" ', unpublished paper given to Australian Society of Association Executives, 1981.

Chapter 12 'The cable decision: underlying issues', in *New Media: Law and Policy*, ed. Mark Armstrong, Faculty of Law, UNSW, Sydney, 1981.

Chapter 13 'Images of cable: The broad social impact of cable TV', *Journal of Media Law and Practice*, vol. 3, no. 3, December 1982.

B. References cited in the text

Allen, G. 1970, *Who Controls the Press?*, American Opinion Reprint, Belmont, Mass.

Armstrong, Mark 1980, 'The Broadcasting and Television Act, 1948–1976: A case study of the Australian Broadcasting Control Board', in *Legislation and Society in Australia*, ed. Roman Tomasic, Sydney

Australian Broadcasting Tribunal 1977, *Self-regulation for Broadcasters?*, AGPS, Canberra

Baer, Walter et al. 1974, *Concentration of Mass Media Ownership: Assessing the State of Current Knowledge*, Rand Corporation Report, Santa Monica

Boehringer, Kathe 1981, 'Gee whiz, or how to think about technological change', in *Media in Crisis*, eds Boehringer et al., Communication, Technology and Control Foundation, Sydney

Bonner, Frances 1982, 'Public assessments of the social impact of the new media technology', paper presented at the Conference of the Sociological Association of Australia and New Zealand

Buckalew, James 1969, 'News elements and selection of television news editors', *Journal of Broadcasting*, vol. 14, no. 1, Winter

Christensen, L. and Ruch, C.E.L. 1978, 'Assessment of brochures and radio and television presentations on hurricane awareness', *Mass Emergencies*, vol. 3, pp. 209–16

Compaine, Benjamin M. 1979, *Who Owns the Media? Concentration of Ownership in the Mass Communications Industry*, Knowledge Industry Publications, White Plains

Comstock, George et al. 1975, *Television and Human Behaviour*, Columbia University Press, New York

Court, John H. 1980, *Pornography: A Christian Critique*, Paternoster Press, Exeter

Curnow, G. R. and Turner, K. 1985, 'Reflections on a colleague', *Politics*, vol. 20, no. 2, pp. 14–19, November

Dominick, Joseph R. and Pearce, Millard C. 1976, 'Trends in network prime-time programming, 1953-74', *Journal of Communication*, vol. 26, no. 1, Winter

Frank, R. and Greenberg, G. 1980, *The Public's Use of Television*, Sage, Beverly Hills

Goot, Murray 1986, *Henry Mayer's 'Immortal Works'. Scholarly, Semi-Scholarly and Not Very Scholarly at All. A Descriptive Bibliography with Index, 1940-1985*, Australasian Political Studies Association, Canberra

Gormley, William T. Jr. 1976, *The Effects of Newspaper-Television Cross Ownership on New Homogeneity,* Institute for Research in Social Science, University of North Carolina, Chapel Hill

Gunaratne, S. 1977, 'Stormy birth leaves Press Council undaunted in Australia', *IPI Report,* March

Harrison, K.M. 1980, 'Public participation in television licencing hearings: should it be continued?', *Science for a Sustainable Society: Communication*, ANZAAS 50th Jubilee Congress, Papers, Adelaide

Henderson, Gerard 1983, *Mr Santamaria and the Bishops*, 2nd revised edn, Hale & Iremonger, Sydney

Horan, Wheeler and Lenehan 1979, *Public Opinion of the ABC*, Sydney

Hunt, Lord 1982, *Report of the Inquiry into Cable Expansion and Broadcasting Policy*, Hunt Report, Home Office, Cmnd 8579, HMSO, London

Keating, Paul 1976, *House of Representatives, Parliamentary Debates*, 4 December

Kueneman, R.M. and Wright, J.E. 1975, 'New policies of broadcast stations for civil disturbances and disasters', *Journalism Quarterly*, p. 52

Larsen, Stein Ugelvik, Hagtvet, Bernt and Myklebust, Jan Peter eds 1980, *Who Were the Fascists: Social Roots of European Fascism*, Universitietsforlarget, Bergen

Lemert, J. 1974, 'Content duplication by the networks in competing evening newscasts', *Journalism Quarterly*, vol. 51, no. 2, September, pp. 238–44

Lull, J. 1980a, 'Family communication patterns and the social uses of Television', *Communication Research*, vol. 7, no. 3, July, pp. 319–34

Lull, J. 1980b, 'The social uses of television', *Human Communication Research*, vol. 6, no. 3, Spring, pp. 197–209

McQuail, D. 1977, *Analysis of Newspaper Content*, Royal Commission on the Press, Research Series 4, HMSO, London

Mayer, Henry 1964, *The Press in Australia*, Lansdowne, Sydney

——1967, 'Introduction', in *Catholics and the Free Society*, ed. Henry Mayer, Cheshire, Melbourne

——1974, 'The media: Strategies for change', paper to the APSA conference, July

——1976a, 'Media: Challenge for change', in *Australian Politics: A Fourth Reader*, eds Henry Mayer and Helen Nelson, Cheshire, Melbourne

——1976b, 'Media' in *Australian Politics: A Fourth Reader*, eds Henry Mayer and Helen Nelson, Cheshire, Melbourne

——1976c, 'What should (and could) we do about the media?', in *Mass Media in Australia*, ed G. Major, Hodder and Stoughton, Sydney

——1985, 'How the media should counter government action', Address to 50th Anniversary Conference of Australian Associated Press

Mayer, Henry with Bettison, Margaret and Keene, Judy 1976, *A Research Guide to Australian Politics and Cognate Subjects*, F. W. Cheshire, Melbourne

Mayer, Henry and Curnow, G.R. 1968, 'Hunting the PM: 33 traits in search of a man', *Australian Quarterly*, vol. 40, no. 1

Mayer, Henry and Kirby, Liz 1984, *A Research Guide to Australian Politics and Cognate Subjects II*, Longman Cheshire, Melbourne

Mayer, Henry, Loveday, Peter and Westerway, Peter 1960, 'Images of politics: An analysis of letters to the press on the Richardson Report', *Australian Journal of Politics and History*, vol. VI, no. 2.

Milne, G. 1977, 'Cyclone Tracy: Some consequences of the evacuation for adult victims', *Australian Psychologist*, vol. 12, no. 1, March

Muggeridge, Malcolm 1977, *Christ and the Media*, Hodder and Stoughton, London

Murray, John 1977, 'Violence in children's television: continuing research issues', *Media Information Australia*, vol. 1, no. 3, February

Murray, John and Kippax, S. 1978, 'Children's social behaviour in three towns with different television experience', *Journal of Communication*, vol. 28, no. 1, pp. 19–29

National Parliament Consultative Committee on the Implications of Telecommunications for Canadian Sovereignty, 1979, *Telecommunications and Canada*, Ottawa

Noelle-Neumann, E. 1974, 'The spiral of silence', *Journal of Communication*, vol. 24, no. 1, Spring

Oost, J. 1979, 'The media and community morale', in *Planning for People in Natural Disaster*, ed. J.I. Reid, Department of Behavioural Sciences, James Cook University, Townsville

Owen, Bruce M. 1978, 'The economic view of programming', *Journal of Communications*, vol. 38, no. 2, Spring

Patkin, Benzion 1980, *The Dunera Internees*, Cassell, Adelaide

Pearl, Cyril 1983, *The Dunera Scandal*, Angus & Robertson, Sydney

Postal and Telecommunications Department 1976, *Australian Broadcasting*, Green Report, AGPS, Canberra

Rosengren, K.E., Arvidson, P. and Sturreson, D. 1975, 'The Barseback "Panic": A radio programme as a negative summary event', *Acta Sociologica*, vol. 18, no. 4

Rosnow, R.C. 1974, 'On rumor', *Journal of Communication*, vol. 24

Scanlon, T.J. 1979, 'Day one in Darwin: once again the vital role of communications', in *Planning for People in Natural Disaster*, ed. J. I. Reid, Department of Behavioural Sciences, James Cook University, Townsville

Scanlon, T.J. 1977, 'Post-disaster rumor chains: a case study', *Mass Emergencies*

Scanlon, T.J., Luukku, R.L. and Morton, G. 1978, 'Media coverage of crises: better than reported, worse than necessary', *Journalism Quarterly*, vol. 55, no. 1, Spring

Semmler, Clement 1981, *The ABC. Aunty Sally and Sacred Cow*, Melbourne University Press, Melbourne

Sloan Commission 1971, *The Television Abundance*, Report of the Sloan Commission on Cable Communications, McGraw-Hill, New York

Smith, A. 1977, *Subsidies and the Press in Europe*, PEP, London

Spero, Robert 1980, *The Duping of the American Voter: Dishonesty and Deception in Presidential Television Advertising*, Doubleday, New York

Sterling, C. and Haight, T. 1978, *The Mass Media: Aspen Institute Guide to Communication Industry Trends*, Praeger, New York

Tuchman, G. 1978, *Making News: A Study in the Construction of Realism*, Free Press, New York

Walmsley, J.D. 1980, 'Spatial bias in the media: an Australian example', ANZAAS 50th Congress, Papers Section 33, Communication, Adelaide

Waxman, J.J. 1973, 'Local broadcast gatekeeping during natural disasters', *Journalism Quarterly*, vol. 50, no. 4, Winter

Western, J. and Hughes, C.A., 1983, *The Mass Media in Australia*, 2nd edn, University of Queensland, St Lucia

Wiltshire, K.W. and Stokes, C.H. 1977a, *Government Regulation and the Electronic Media Industry*, CEDA, Melbourne and Sydney

——1977b, *Government Regulation and the Printed Media Industry*, CEDA, Melbourne and Sydney

Index